JESUS

STANLEY SOLANA

© EDIMAT BOOKS Ltd. London
is an affiliate of Edimat Libros S.A.
C/ Primavera, 35 Pol. Ind. El Malvar
Arganda del Rey - 28500 (Madrid) Spain
E-mail: edimat@edimat.es

Title: *Jesus*
Author: *Stanley Solana*

ISBN: 84-9794-014-8
Legal Deposit: M-48406-2004

PRINTED IN SPAIN

INTRODUCTION

Palestine before Jesus

Palestine had long forgotten the glorious times of Israel. It was primarily a nation of craftsmen, farmers, fishermen, shepherds and other persons engaged in trade and religious enterprises. Most of them were reputed for their skill and, in certain cases, could even be considered brilliant. As for the monotheistic religion inherited from Moses and Solomon, great divisions could be perceived. Orthodox Jews comprised the large majority, yet Zealots, Sadducees and the Qumran Essenians could all be found in the mountains.

The name Palestine itself was a sort of insult imposed by the dominating Romans, as it was bestowed based on the Philistin (Philistines), the age-old enemies of the Jews. When the latter were defeated, the nation was called Canaan. Later it came to be known as Judea, after Judah, which was the most important of the tribes of Israel.

These lands included an area called Galilee, where Jesus preached his most important sermons as an adult and where people could gaze at their reflections in an enormous, blue lake. Many of the inhabitants of the area were poorly educated fisherman, who gave themselves away by their peculiar way of speaking or, should we say, their accent. It was a very green and fertile land, which also happened to be farmed by a people who were waiting for a voice that would teach them a more 'loving' and 'mutually supportive' religion than the official creed enforced by Jerusalem.

Samaria, the rich and heretic land that concentrated all its interest in the mountain of Siquem, since they still believed that Yahweh should be worshipped here and not in the temple at Jerusalem, is deserving of an altogether different mention. Jesus often passed through here, and it was home to a number of his followers.

The meek Jews

The proud Jews we read about in the Bible under the command of King David, or those governed by King Solomon, the wisest and most powerful monarch in the world, had become more submissive. Their own internal divisions, perhaps fostered by the existence of twelve tribes since the days of Jacob, had ended up weakening the country. It was already a Roman colony, although Herod enjoyed a certain amount of political hegemony, at least for local decisions.

Some historians have uncovered the surprising fact that there were more Jews outside Palestine than within the country itself. In fact, the successive invasions of the territory, which at times lasted for centuries, had favoured the creation of large Jewish colonies in the Mediterranean basin. In the days of Moses, the largest of such colonies was to be found in Egypt, although it is difficult to tell where the most prosperous of these colonies was at this time.

We are certain that powerful Jewish families lived in Rome, where they continued to practice their rituals and maintain their ancient customs. However, they were well settled in the capital. The greatest traders and ship owners were also Jewish, although there is nothing that would lead us to believe they intended to use their money, or even a part of it, to free Palestine.

The importance of the priests

The laws of Moses were solid as a rock, no concessions were made. They were based on wide-reaching principles, compulsory rituals and were exclusively controlled by the priests. This converted the holy men into dictators, able to impose strict control throughout the entire country. As we mentioned above, there were many religious divisions, perhaps explaining why the Sanhedrin, the group of priests-judges, had become so authoritarian.

Jesus and the fishermen (drawing by Rembrandt)

They did not hesitate to send out their spies to the far corners of Palestine in order to prevent new conflicts from breaking out. When Jesus began to preach, he was watched at all times, in the hope that he would make his final mistake. We will speak about this in later chapters.

The issue of the Messiah

The Aramaic word *meschiah* means 'the anointed one'. Its Greek translation is Khristos, which is why Jesus was given this name. However, many kings, such as David, patriarchs, prophets and high priests received the name Messiah. Israel had been waiting for him, but a series of failures due to certain impostors delayed the appearance of the true Messiah.

Remarkably, Jesus fulfilled all the requirements to be considered the one, true Messiah. If the prophet Isaiah said, "there shall come forth a shoot from the stump of Jesse, and a branch shall grow out of his roots," this prophecy was fulfilled in the son of Mary and Joseph, as he was a direct descendant of King David's family. There was also truth in the prophetic Psalm which claimed, "But you, O Bethlehem Ephrathah, who are little to be among the clans of Judah, from you shall come forth for me one who is to be ruler in Israel," as Jesus was born in this town.

Despite all of this, the Jews who were in favour of the government did not grant Jesus the status of Messiah. They did not even listen to him when he admitted to being such. It would be up to his disciples and, later, half of the world, to grant him a rank that only he deserved.

Despite its insignificance

When reading Roman historians of the time, such as Tacitus, we can see that Israel was considered an insignificant colony.

However, the world's three primary monotheistic religions, Judaism, Christianity and Islam, were born in that land. It is true that the latter emerged in another country, but the Koran could never have been written without the Bible. In addition, many of the main characters in the latter play a part, insignificant as it may be, in the Islamic text. Grundmann fittingly points out the following:

Jesus teaching (drawing by Rembrandt)

Humanity owes Israel the belief in a God that created and maintains heaven and earth and that governs the fate of his people and mankind as a whole, who cannot be represented or fully grasped, who is not a part of the world, but is above it and governs it. Israel bears witness to the fact that this God is its ally, and that he made them the people of his Alliance, revealed himself to them and showed them his will through his holy commandments.

This was how Israel opened the doors to the other two religions. In order for Christianity to appear, it was necessary for the Son of Man, Jesus, who gave up his doctrine and his life for mankind, to be born in that land, although surprisingly, it could only escape across the Mediterranean.

The structure of this book

It would seem that everyone who has set about writing a biography of Jesus would have to have begun with the four official gospels, contributions from the Apocrypha and other texts as a base. In actual fact, the work is quite complicated, as no logical timeline exists: the Evangelists narrate different events, although they are all an attempt to reflect the life of Jesus. They describe some events of great importance which others ignore, yet each of them provides exclusive new perspectives.

We have followed a story line we believe to be logical, although we cannot be sure that we have faithfully respected the timeline. What we tried to keep in mind was a reflection of Jesus the Man, without forgetting his most important actions and while introducing some further contributions, based on new discoveries in the field of archaeology.

Nevertheless, at no time is it our intention to indoctrinate, because the motto of our collection, which is being respected by all our authors, is to provide a well-documented biography, with a pleasant literary style, so that you may continue researching on your own if you so desire. As a nudge in the right direction we have provided a complete Bibliography below.

So, we hope that the following pages will entertain you and, especially, that it will arouse your interest in the subject.

Bibliography

ABECASSIS, ELIETTE: *Qumran*

BARREAU, JEAN CLAUDE: *Biographie de Jésus*

BENÍTEZ, J. J.: *Los astronautas de Yavé (Yahweh's astronauts)*

CANNON, DOLORES: *Jesús y los esenios (Jesus and the Essenians)*

CLARE PROPHET, ELIZABETH: *The Lost Years of Jesus*

DODD, CHARLES HAROLD: *The Founder of Christianity*

DOMINIC CROSSAN, JOHN: *The Historical Jesus: The Life of a Mediterranean Jewish Peasant*

DUFOUR, XAVIER-LEÓN: *Les Evangiles et l'Histoire de Jésus (The gospels and the History of Jesus)*

FRICKE, WEDDIG: *The Court-Martial of Jesus*

HASSNAIN, FIDA: *A Search for the Historical Jesus*

KÄSEMANN, ERNST: *The Problem of the Historical Jesus*

LUDWIG, EMIL: *The Son of Man*

MACK, BURTON L.: *The Lost Gospel – The Book of Q & Christian Origins*

MARTÍN, SANTIAGO: *El evangelio secreto de la Virgen María (The Secret Gospel of the Virgin Mary)*

MARTÍN DESCALZO, JOSÉ LUIS: *Vida y misterio de Jesús de Nazaret (Life And Mystery of Jesus of Nazareth)*

MAURIAC, FRANÇOIS: *Vie de Jésus (Jesus' life)*

MICHA, ALEXANDRE: *Les Enfances du Christ (The Gospels of the childhood of Christ)*

PERROT, CHARLES: *Jésus et l'histoire (Jesus and History)*
RENAN, ERNEST: *The Life of Jesus*
ROBBINS, VICTORIA: *The Enigma of the Biblical Texts*
ROPS, DANIEL: *Jésus en son temps (Jesus in his Time)*
ROUX, JEAN-PAUL: *Jésus*
SCHILLEBEECKX, EDWARD: *The Historical Figure of Jesus*
SCHURE, EDOUARD: *Los grandes iniciados: Jesús, Hermes, Krishna, Moisés, Orfeo, Pitágoras, Platón y Rama (The great initiated: Jesus, Hermes, Krishna, Moses, Orpheus, Pythagorus, Plato and Ramases)*
SCHWEITZER, ALBERT: *The Quest of the Historical Jesus*
THIEDE, CARSTEN PETER; D'ANCONA, MATTHEW: *The Jesus Papyrus*
VERMES, GEZA: *Dead Sea Scrolls*

THE NEW OXFORD ANNOTATED BIBLE (Revised Standard Version)

CHAPTER I
SON OF A VIRGIN

A 15-year-old woman

Mary, the daughter of Joachim and Anna, had just turned fifteen and she had never had sexual relations with any man. For whatever reason, she had decided to keep her virginity, although this was never the greatest of her priorities. She had enough work already with the household chores, helping in the fields and keeping the strict religious rules.

She could not be considered beautiful, although there was certainly something attractive in her eyes and face, more due to the respect and seriousness they inspired than anything else. What truly surprised everyone was how soon she had matured. She was rarely seen to be wasting time, even when she was a girl. It could be said that there were not enough hours in the day for her to carry out her duties, which was why she insisted on completing them as soon as possible, without rushing. She also knew how to anticipate her parents' orders, which should not be seen as extraordinary as she was never idle nor seemed to tire. Another of her gifts was her constant smile, for just watching a new sunrise filled her with happiness.

Since she was used to the oral traditions of Israel, she respected them all except for one, which was the tendency of great women to surround themselves with children of their own. Mary liked children, especially those of her many cousins.

One day, she found that she was to be married to Joseph, the young carpenter. She knew him very well since, in the small village of Nazareth, where they had both lived since they were born, everyone knew of the deeds and activities of their neighbours.

Peculiarly, in that rural society, as in all of Israel, marriage did not oblige the spouses to live together. They could continue to live with their parents if they so desired. However, they did enter into a commitment of absolute faithfulness. The situation changed whenever a child was born, because then the couple had to come together to raise the child with the greatest possible dedication.

The visit of the angel Gabriel

Mary was very solemn when she woke up that morning. Yet as she immediately washed and went to the small kitchen to make her parents' breakfast, as they were going on a journey, nobody could appreciate the change. As she watched them leave, she already had the clothes she was going to wash in her hands.

Hours later, while she was sewing inside the house, a bright light made her look forwards. At that moment she saw a youth dressed in shining white, watching her with a bright smile. One would have expected the Nazarene girl to fall from her chair, overcome by panic, and then try to stammer a few questions: "Who are you? How did you get in? What do you want from me?"

However, she simply stood up, apparently not afraid, as if she was receiving a visit she had been expecting from the time she was born. This was why she joyfully received the message of the Annunciation:

"Hail, O favoured one, the Lord is with you! Behold, you will conceive in your womb and bear a son, and you shall call

16

his name Jesus. He will be great, and will be called the Son of the Most High; and the Lord God will give to him the throne of his father David, and he will reign over the house of Jacob for ever; and of his kingdom there will be no end."

Mary had been prepared to hear these words, which were of such colossal importance that she remained silent for several minutes. Her human mind needed time to process all the information. Then logic, in a development that was completely unreal due to its divine nature, led her to ask the following question:

"How shall this be, since I have no husband?"

The angel Gabriel had the most soothing answer:

"The Holy Spirit will come upon you, and the power of the Most High will overshadow you; therefore the child to be born will be called holy, the Son of God. And behold, your kinswoman Elizabeth in her old age has also conceived a son; and this is the sixth month with her who was called barren. For with God nothing will be impossible."

Although these words would have been incomprehensible to any other woman, Mary understood them at once, even though the weight of such a responsibility forced her to kneel down. Never before had she felt stronger. Her posture was an act of respectful submission, which she proved with the following sentences:

"Behold, I am the handmaid of the Lord. Let it be to me according to your word."

This was how the sublime incident ended, while the bright light faded away and the angel disappeared into thin air, with no need to pass through wall or roof. He had delivered his message, and a very singular life was germinating in Mary's womb.

Minutes later, she came out of her trance with a happy expression on her face, until reality led her to realise that she could not tell anyone about what had happened. Who would believe her? She was a poor young girl, with no apparent mer-

17

its that would grant her the right to be visited by an angel, who had announced to her that she would be the 'mother of the Son of God'... Her neighbours would think she had gone mad if she told them what had just happened.

The best thing she could do was to keep quiet about the great event. Later on she would find a solution to such a compromising situation.

The old cousin Elizabeth

Mary awaited the return of her parents with no sign of unease. She had never lied to them, nor was she planning on doing so. She did not hesitate to tell them about the prodigy, and they believed her from the start. It is possible that there was communication on a level of sensitivity, a shared emotion or, on a more common plain, that her parents were unable to believe that such a simple and honest mind as that of their daughter could come up with such a fabulous lie.

The fact of the matter is that there was an almost immediate understanding between the three of them. In the meantime, hugs sealed a pact of silence; no one should hear about the pregnancy. When Mary announced that she wished to go and see her cousin Elizabeth on her own she was not denied this right, which was hers through the announcement of the angel. It would be the first time she had left Nazareth, to travel to Judea, a three-day journey. In her parents' eyes she had become a superior woman, someone who was able to face up to any danger, since he who had granted her the gift of divine motherhood had ensured that suitable protection would be provided. Nevertheless, they gave her some advice and prepared some provisions for the way.

In any case, six months earlier, the notable Rabbi Zechariah had received an amazing visit in the temple. He had been about to leave, after performing all his duties, when he was dazzled by the presence of the angel Gabriel. As though he had been struck by lightning, the old man fell to the floor and covered his face with his hands, trembling in panic.

"Do not be afraid, Zechariah, for your prayer is heard, and your wife Elizabeth will bear you a son, and you shall call his name John. He will make ready for the Lord a people prepared."

Mary visiting her cousin Elizabeth at the happiest of moments

The rabbi found this revelation so incredible that he hesitated for a few seconds, unable to understand how the favour was being offered to him now that he was an old man instead of when he was still young.

And the angel Gabriel announced, "Behold, you will be silent and unable to speak until the day that these things come to pass, because you did not believe my words."

And this is what came to pass, though the rabbi felt no resentment, since the reward he would receive well deserved such punishment, which would prevent him from performing his duties in the temple. He had nine months of performing lesser tasks ahead of him, while he communicated with the faithful in writing and, especially, through middlemen who could read.

A joyful meeting

It is possible that Mary covered the path between Nazareth and Judea on a donkey, with saddlebags containing provisions for the traveller and some gifts for her cousins. The path seemed short to her, since her mind was so occupied with her plans for the future.

The spring sunshine greeted her when she entered the city, and she was filled with joy when she dismounted. Through the open door of the house she could see her old cousin with her freshly combed long, grey hair, looking at her swollen womb. A smile lit up her face, and her whole person seemed to be a song of happiness.

"My dear Elizabeth," exclaimed Mary, feeling closer to the woman than ever.

Elizabeth turned around immediately, an expression of admiration on her face, and unable to contain herself, greeted Mary as follows:

"Blessed are you among women, and blessed is the fruit of your womb! And why is this granted me, that the mother of my Lord should come to me? For behold, when the voice of your greeting came to my ears, the babe in my womb leaped for joy."

In order to show that she shared Elizabeth's happiness, Mary intoned a magnificent song, which was born from the inspiration she received from the child being formed in her womb:

My soul magnifies the Lord,
and my spirit rejoices in God my Saviour,
for he has regarded the low estate of his handmaiden.
For behold, henceforth all generations will call me blessed;
for he who is mighty has done great things for me,
and holy is his name.
And his mercy is on those who fear him
from generation to generation.
He has shown strength with his arm,
he has scattered the proud in the imagination of their hearts,
he has put down the mighty from their thrones,
and exalted those of low degree;
he has filled the hungry with good things,
and the rich he has sent empty away.
He has helped his servant Israel,
in remembrance of his mercy,
as he spoke to our fathers,
to Abraham and to his posterity for ever."

This song would be called the 'Magnificat'. It is surprising that it came from a fifteen-year-old girl, who was probably illiterate, despite having been educated with great religious culture, since she never forgot anything she heard, in particular religious traditions. Yet if we are to believe that she was in the first weeks of divine motherhood, we can accept any lesser ability.

Mary stayed with her cousins for three months. A few days after he was born, the child was to be circumcised, as tradition dictated. Then, the mother wanted to call the child John. All her relatives were opposed to this idea since none of them, not even their ancestors, had been called by this name. Faced with the mother's stubbornness, as she could not go against the orders of the angel Gabriel, they turned to Zechariah.

He wrote the chosen name on a piece of paper, to prove that he was able to speak it aloud: 'John'. He had recovered his voice, with which the collective enthusiasm became even greater. From that moment nobody was opposed to the child being called John.

That same night, however, Mary and Elizabeth exchanged a very solemn gaze. They did not need to put into words what was worrying them both: 'How would Joseph the carpenter react when he learned his future wife was pregnant?' Was he in a position to accept the intervention of the Holy Spirit? And in the event that he refused to marry Mary, would she be stoned as an adulteress?

Joseph, a tolerant man

Israeli law was very strict with women who committed adultery. Although Mary had not married Joseph, they became an official couple on the day they announced their engagement and therefore, both of them, especially the woman, were bound to respect marital fidelity.

When she returned to Nazareth, Mary met with Joseph, who had missed her all the while. He loved her deeply, so much that he kissed her hands when helping her down from her donkey. They then went together to visit her parents, and then she bathed, changed clothes and ate. She no longer worried about her responsibility since she was sure she had the support of the carpenter, however…

"You must believe me, Joseph," Mary repeated for the third time. "I am with child of the Holy Spirit."

"I should believe you because I love you, woman... My heart tells me you are unable to lie... Of course I am a man... People are aware that we have not been together in the last three months... And I know we have never shared a bed..."

"I am going to be the mother of the Son of God, Joseph."

The carpenter was deaf to any explanation. Unable to think, since the confession he had just heard had completely overwhelmed him, he left the house. He walked aimlessly for hours. He was illiterate, did not go to the temple often, because work was hard to come by, and when he had the chance, he had to take it, forgetting his religious commitments.

Joseph could not help but doubt the truth of Mary's pregnancy

23

Another thing that weighed on his mind was the sexist concept that he had not 'tried' Mary, whom he loved more than his own life. Finally, he decided to break off the engagement, leaving her free. But, what would people think when they found out she was going to have a child? In a few months she would not be able to hide her swollen belly...

"I must protect her," he told himself, full of uncertainty. "If she marries me she will not be in danger. But I will still have my doubts... What must I do?"

Sleep came to him well into the night. Once he went to bed, restless, unable to stop tossing and turning, the angel Gabriel appeared to him in a dream and told him:

"Joseph, son of David, do not fear to take Mary your wife, for that which is conceived in her is of the Holy Spirit; she will bear a son, and you shall call his name Jesus, for he will save his people from their sins."

The carpenter was then able to sleep peacefully. The next morning, he donned his finest clothes and went to the house of his future in-laws to ask them for Mary's hand in marriage. He was granted his wish immediately, and the future couple left to occupy what would be their new house. As soon as they crossed the threshold, the marriage was complete. They were already husband and wife in their own eyes and in those of society. However, they slept in separate beds until the Son of God was born.

The 'logic' of the legend

We will consider as legend the numerous apocryphal gospels, the stacks of 'unofficial' writings as well as any other literature that is 'not accepted by the Vatican'. There is a 'logical' version of the story to explain Joseph's behaviour from a more human perspective.

In this case, the carpenter is shown as a very mature man, with Mary as his second wife. He would have had several children from his first marriage, which would explain why some of the gospels point at the possibility of Jesus having older brothers and sisters.

A man who has known other women, who is also old enough to be able to do without sex, is more able to accept living with a virgin. A virgin who continued to be so until the day she died, in other words, until she was almost one hundred years old.

However, imagining that Joseph was resigned to loving his wife platonically implies a certain effort due to the exceptional nature of such a task. He lived by her side, they shared a house and at many times even a bed, yet he never had carnal relations with her. The image is of a sublime romanticism, typical of the knights-errant of the Middle Ages.

The truth is that the couple had to confront a great many problems, due to which they had scarce time to think of themselves. They took on the role of the parents of the Son of God, and they would only be able to look after him for a few years. Soon enough they would see him gain independence and find his own way, while they stayed at home waiting for news. They were afraid to discover the fate that awaited him, a fate that took its time to become apparent, because he had not yet come into the world.

The prophecy came true

Recent investigations have revealed that Mary and Joseph did not go to Bethlehem to fill out a compulsory enrolment, as Israel was not a Roman province at the time. They did not arrive in December either, but rather in the spring.

The choice of Bethlehem was made by Zechariah, for he was a rabbi after all. After the visits from the angels, the surprising birth of his son John and the announcement that Mary was to be the mother of the Son of God, he decided that the prophecy of Micah should come true:

But you, O Bethlehem of Ephrathah, who are little to be among the clans of Judah, from you shall come forth for me one who is to be ruler in Israel.

The distance between Nazareth and Bethlehem is about one hundred miles, over particularly rough terrain. It is certain that the couple used a donkey, as well as the fact that they bore a small load. At the different stages on the way they sheltered themselves with the open sky, a thick tree, a rocky wall, or any other form of natural protection.

Humble people never thought about midwifes, let alone doctors, since the women who were closest at the time helped in childbirth, generally the greatest experts in the family. In this case they expected to have some kind of divine help.

When they reached their destination, they found that the small city and its surrounding villages were engaged in a large celebration. All the inns were full. However, a great number of tents had been pitched and caves and farmyards had been fitted out to be used as provisional homes. This was normal practice at the time, especially during the celebration of large feasts such as Passover.

Mary and Joseph were able to occupy one of these provisional houses, one of the last ones, just when they feared they would have to sleep outdoors. The birth of Jesus was only hours away. We are convinced that many people assisted Mary in childbirth, since this custom was deeply rooted in those lands, something as sacred as the ancient obligation of helping any shipwrecked person while at sea.

CHAPTER II

THE GREATEST EVENT OF AN ERA

The Son of God is born

The families that were close to Mary and Joseph at the time Jesus was born were shepherd families. The men lit fires, and the women took to boiling water and ensuring plenty of clean cloths were available, which they used as towels and bandages as required.

"He is coming..." whispered the sweet Nazarene woman, showing no sign of pain.

The arrival of Jesus in this world took place as if he had emerged from the most precious treasure chest: a ray of sun incarnate, filling the cave with light, completely clean from blood and remains of placenta, and free of the umbilical cord. He was in the hands of the woman who assisted Mary, with his eyes open, moving his small hands. It was a miracle that the woman did not drop him, since she was overwhelmed at witnessing such a unique moment.

Since the cave-stable was filled with light, those present knew the newborn would be a great man. It was a real show, worthy of feeding the fieriest of legends, such as that Jean-Paul Roux includes in his book *Jesus of Nazareth*:

The Proto-Gospel of James tells of a blinding light filling the cave in Bethlehem. After it faded away Jesus appeared, which is like saying that the light was co-substantial to him, or that it was one of his epiphanies. The legend, less true than its details, develops by saying that Joseph innocently went to search for a midwife for Mary. He found one and took her to his wife, and the woman stopped at the door to the cave. And a shining cloud covered this cave, and the midwife said, "My spirit has been glorified today, for my eyes have seen wonders." And the cave suddenly filled with such intense clarity that the human eye could not contemplate it. And when this light had gradually faded away, they saw the child. Mary, his mother, was feeding him. And the midwife exclaimed, "This is a great day for me, for I have seen a sublime sight. And she left the cavern and met Salome. And the midwife said to Salome, "I have great news for you: a virgin has given birth and remained virgin."

This legend should not be considered too exaggerated, as it is essentially similar to St. John's writings in the Gospel:

And the Word became flesh and dwelt among us, full of grace and truth; we have beheld his glory, glory as of the only Son from the Father.

These extremely hermetic terms that are best read by initiates or theologians are much better represented by popular literature, though it might often include elements of fantasy. Essentially, Jesus' birth was an event of universal importance and this is proven by archaeology, astronomy and other sciences.

The Magi were not kings

Many historians do not see the Magi as kings, but consider them to have been wise astronomers or astrologers. They were probably the latter, as in those times the movements of the stars were observed to read destiny. Babylon was the centre of astrology and there had been Jewish scientists there since the times of Daniel.

The birth of Jesus in Bethlehem

The Three Wise Men are thought to have been Jewish astrologers living in Babylon. Only those who knew of the 'conjunction of Moses' and the meaning of its repetition would feel so excited when they saw the 'star'. They immediately 'read' the message and set off for Palestine. However, it is hard to believe that the star actually marked their path like a traffic sign, as their true guide was their knowledge of their cultural traditions. They therefore got to Jerusalem and went to consult Herod. They would have had no need to do this had they had a moving star to guide them.

W. Otto states that the sect of the Pharisees was where it was held most strongly that the Messiah would appear in Palestine; meanwhile, the people were convinced that Herod's reign was about to end, as "soon the divine sign we are awaiting will appear."

Archaeological excavations carried out by Schnabel in Babylon revealed tablets of cuneiform script registering that Sippar astrologers had observed the conjunction of Jupiter and Saturn in Pisces over five months in 7 BC. Not being Jewish, they might not have felt anything out of the ordinary. Their reaction was very different to that of the three wise men that walked all through January. They took about forty-five days to reach Jerusalem, and must have got there towards the end of February or during the first week of March.

The Gospels tell us that there were a series of meetings between the Magi and Herod, which could well have taken twenty days, until it was known that the 'child king of Israel' would be born in Bethlehem, about five miles away from Jerusalem. However, on 14th March, the third conjunction of the planets took place, and must have been observed by the Jewish astrologers from Babylon. It filled them with joy.

The slaughter of the innocents

Modern historians take 'Herod the Great' as their reference. There is enough information existing to place Jesus' birth. The Gospels say that he ruled at this time and this is surprising, because he died in April of the year 4 BC. There must be a mistake somewhere.

Herod ordered all children in Bethlehem under the age of two to be killed. If we take this into account, we have to shift the date of this tragedy to 8 or 7 BC. Josephus, the historian of the Jews, does not mention it in his writings, but there is a very believable testimony in Macrobius, in his biography of Augustus in 400 AD. He used a great many documents as his references that have since been lost, some of which tell of the slaughter of the innocents ordered by Herod. This must situate us in about 8 or 7 BC.

In the Gospel according to St. Matthew (2:16-18) we read the following:

Then Herod, when he saw that he had been tricked by the wise men, was in a furious rage, and he sent and killed all the male children in Bethlehem and in all that region who were two years old or under, according to the time which he had ascertained from the wise men. Then was fulfilled what was spoken by the prophet Jeremiah: "A voice was heard in Ramah, wailing and loud lamentation, Rachel weeping for her children; she refused to be consoled, because they were no more."

This passage makes reference to the historical moment when Sargon took the people of Israel into exile. Rachel was the mother of several of the main tribes, those of Ephraim, Manases and Benjamin, and so the metaphor of weeping for

31

her 'children' should be seen as a logical metaphor. Ramah was a town of Benjamin where Rachel's tomb was said to lie.

Herod's terror

When the long awaited 'star of Moses' appeared in the year 7 BC, it shone so brightly that some astronomers were able to see it. Nothing like this had happened when other stars appeared in the sky in 126 and 66 BC, as they came up in the late hours of the afternoon when the sun's rays made it impossible to see them, or at midday, when it would have been even more difficult.

The conjunction of 7 BC, therefore, must be seen as a very special sign, especially as it was repeated on 29th May, 3rd October and 14th January. The astronomers no longer had any doubt that they were confronting the announcement of the coming of the Messiah!

In Israel, this event was definitely expected. When the Three Wise Men went to Herod to ask about the recently born King of the Jews, the scriptures tell us that the cruel monarch was terrified, as was the whole of Jerusalem.

He nevertheless probably only felt afraid because he was a foreigner. The news led him to believe he would lose his position, and so he behaved astutely, at the beginning, and later, when he found out that the three Magi had not told him of the child's birth, with terrible cruelty.

The historian W. Otto has proven that in the year 6 BC the idea of the coming of the Messiah was alive among the Jews. Important groups arose that fervently believed this and hoped to make it come true as soon as possible. Herod disbanded them with severe punishments. Afterwards, he was on the alert, and the announcement of the three Magi only served to confirm that his fears were true.

Very few doubted the star of the Three Wise Men

The presence of the Three Wise Men in Bethlehem can be considered historically true in view of all the information available on it. Oswald Gerhardt strongly supports this idea, as do other atheist experts. Richard Henning writes:

The Wise Men in the stable in Bethlehem

Historians cannot give a sure answer as to the mystery of whether or not the wise men were present at the foot of Jesus' cradle. It could be that legend has added a lot of poetic detail to the event. But one thing does seem to be sure, that can be summed up as follows: "The astronomical phenomenon mentioned in the second chapter of the Gospel according to Saint Matthew must be taken as a real historical event, and its astrological interpretation cannot be any other than a newly born king of the Jews seeing the light of the world." The reality of the killing of the children of Bethlehem is proven by the testimony of Macrobius, we can fully affirm that the second chapter of the Gospel of Saint Matthew can be generally considered to be true in everything concerning the story of the Wise Men of the East.

CHAPTER III

JESUS' TRAINING

The flight to Egypt

In the Gospel according to Matthew (2:13-15) we can read:

Now when they had departed, behold, an angel of the Lord appeared to Joseph in a dream and said, "Rise, take the child and his mother, and flee to Egypt, and remain there till I tell you; for Herod is about to search for the child, to destroy him." And he rose and took the child and his mother by night, and departed to Egypt, and remained there until the death of Herod. This was to fulfil what the Lord had spoken by the prophet, "Out of Egypt I have called my son."

This phrase is from a verse by Hosea, given a messianic meaning by Matthew. Certain historians have taken into consideration the fact that the evangelist liked to quote the Old Testament to relate Jesus' return to that of Moses who had been in Egypt. Whether or not Mary, Joseph and the child spent any time in the land of the Nile is doubtful. We prefer to think that the reference is an allegory.

What is accepted, however, is the flight, which could have led anywhere Herod and his Roman friends' influence was not felt. We do not know how long this exile from Palestine lasted either. Meanwhile, the child killer went about his business, killing Mariam, one of his wives, and the two children she had given him. He is also said to have killed other children of his own, including Antipater, the eldest. He had fourteen children with his different wives, and more with his concubines.

Herod divided his kingdom among three of his children, Archelaus, Antipas and Philip. He might have done so when he felt death approaching, as he had quite a few illnesses, the least serious being a stroke. When his end came, danger disappeared for Jesus. Then, as the Gospel of Matthew tells us (2:19-23):

But when Herod died, behold, an angel of the Lord appeared in a dream to Joseph in Egypt, saying, "Rise, take the child and his mother, and go to the land of Israel, for those who sought the child's life are dead." And he rose and took the child and his mother, and went to the land of Israel. But when he heard that Archelaus reigned in Judea in place of his father Herod, he was afraid to go there, and being warned in a dream he withdrew to the district of Galilee. And he went and dwelt in a city called Nazareth, that what was spoken by the prophets might be fulfilled, "He shall be called a Nazarene."

This new quote from the Old Testament that Matthew used is difficult to find for Isaac Asimov, unless there is a mistake and the evangelist is referring to a 'man from Nazareth'. If so, a reference can be found in which an angel tells Samson's mother that she is going to conceive a divine child. The words of the angel are:

"...The man will be a Nazarene of God from his mother's womb and he will be the first to free Israel from the hands of the Philistines."

In this message the fate of Jesus is told, and Matthew highlighted it in his apparent constant concern to make his writings transcendental or messianic.

The gospel according to Luke

Legend has it that there were twenty gospels in all – a dilemma for the leaders of the Church. The different versions did not coincide in many aspects and so they were left on an altar so that 'innocent hands' could shake them. Sixteen of them fell to the floor, and the four that remained on the table were chosen by divine intervention.

Not much credit is given to this legend, but we do have to admit that the four Gospels that have been passed on to us which, together with other texts, make up the New Testament, are mutually contradictory in many aspects.

For example, in the Gospel according to Luke, no mention is made of the presence of the Three Wise Men, and there is no star, no killing of the innocent, nor any flight into Egypt. These questions are too important to be ignored. The theologians' response to this is that "The Gospels complement each other; therefore what is told by one of them should not be taken as a rejection of information given in another, but as new information, another way of setting out sacred events."

We are prepared to accept any comment, but still intend to state palpable evidence. It is hard to believe that events that were so important in the life of Christ, the creator of one of the most important, perhaps the most influential, doctrines in the history of mankind, do not deserve at least a few lines from the other evangelists. This might simply be due to the fact that the gospels were written separately, like the Apocryphal Gospels – none of their writers knew what the others were speaking about. They also took the places where they were writing and their possible audiences strongly into account.

Luke does not mention the flight into Egypt nor the death threat that hung over the baby Jesus, he presents the holy family in Bethlehem and Jerusalem. This interesting fact is told to us as follows (Luke 2:21-24):

And at the end of eight days, when he was circumcised, he was called Jesus, the name given by the angel before he was conceived in the womb.

And when the time came for their purification according to the law of Moses, they brought him up to Jerusalem to present him to the Lord (as it is written in the law of the Lord, "Every male that opens the womb shall be called holy to the Lord") and to offer a sacrifice according to what is said in the law of the Lord, "a pair of turtledoves, or two young pigeons."

This leaves Jesus' Jewish origins clear, even though some historians have questioned them. Matthew does not mention these rituals in his texts, but takes Jesus straight to Egypt to save him from the threat of Herod. We are told to understand these 'purposeful omissions' as a complement to the Sacred Story, and so we will use this as our tactic.

The prophecies of Simeon and Anna

In the Gospel according to Luke (2:25-46), other circumstances are narrated that deserve consideration:

Now there was a man in Jerusalem, whose name was Simeon, and this man was righteous and devout, looking for the consolation of Israel, and the Holy Spirit was upon him. And it had been revealed to him by the Holy Spirit that he should not see death before he had seen the Lord's Christ. And inspired by the Spirit he came into the temple; and when the parents brought in the child Jesus, to do for him accord-

ing to the custom of the law, he took him up in his arms and blessed God and said,

"Lord, now lettest thou thy servant depart in peace, according to thy word; for mine eyes have seen thy salvation which thou hast prepared in the presence of all peoples, a light for revelation to the Gentiles, and for glory to thy people Israel."

And his father and his mother marvelled at what was said about him; and Simeon blessed them and said to Mary his mother.

Jesus speaking with the wise doctors in the temple

"Behold, this child is set for the fall and rising of many in Israel, and for a sign that is spoken against (and a sword will pierce through your own soul also), that thoughts out of many hearts may be revealed."

And there was a prophetess, Anna, the daughter of Phanuel, of the tribe of Asher; she was of a great age, having lived with her husband seven years from her virginity, and as a widow till she was eighty-four. She did not depart from the temple, worshiping with fasting and prayer night and day. And coming up at that very hour she gave thanks to God, and spoke of him to all who were looking for the redemption of Jerusalem.

And when they had performed everything according to the law of the Lord, they returned into Galilee, to their own city, Nazareth. And the child grew and became strong, filled with wisdom; and the favour of God was upon him.

The more we read and re-read the biblical texts from both the Old and New Testaments, the more we understand that they were written for people with a very simple or primary outlook. We are told that Jesus' parents were amazed at the words Simeon spoke, giving the idea that they did not know of their son's fate. But an angel had come to Mary to announce to her that she was going to conceive without having intercourse, because "He will be great, and will be called the Son of the Most High; and the Lord God will give to him the throne of his father David, and he will reign over the house of Jacob for ever; and of his kingdom there will be no end."

Was this not a more grandiose announcement than Simeon's words?

The presence of minor prophets is a clear indication of a desire to show Jesus' life from a human perspective, in line with the traditions of Israel – as if the evangelists had to confirm that the people had the Messiah among them and this made it worth their while to die or to have worked themselves to exhaustion in order to have the honour of seeing the child that "would liberate them".

We must point out here that though there are testimonies to the existence of Herod, the star of the Three Wise Men and the killing of innocent children and that these events therefore have historical value, this is not the case with what Luke tells. Few of the moments in the life of Christ can be 'archaeologically proven', thus making belief in the events quoted in the four Gospels purely a question of faith.

...That I would be here, in my Father's House...

In the Gospel according to Luke (2:41-52), the following events are presented:

Now his parents went to Jerusalem every year at the feast of the Passover. And when he was twelve years old, they went up according to custom; and when the feast was ended, as they were returning, the boy Jesus stayed behind in Jerusalem. His parents did not know it, but supposing him to be in the company they went a day's journey, and they sought him among their kinsfolk and acquaintances; and when they did not find him, they returned to Jerusalem, seeking him. After three days they found him in the temple, sitting among the teachers, listening to them and asking them questions; and all who heard him were amazed at his understanding and his answers. And when they saw him they were astonished; and his mother said to him, "Son, shy have you treated us so? Behold, your father and I have been looking for you anxiously." And he said to them, "How is it that you sought me? Did you not know that I must be in my Father's house?" And they did not understand the saying which he spoke to them. And he went down with them and came to Nazareth, and was obedient to them; and his mother kept all these things in her heart.

41

And Jesus increased in wisdom and in stature, and in favour with God and man.

These words "I must be in my Father's house" seem to show that Jesus needed to make contact with wise men to discuss religious concerns. However, we do not believe that he would settle for just three or four days, that would leave him in his family's hands until...when?

The Gospels mention that when Jesus met John the Baptist he was already thirty years old. What did he do for the eighteen years from when he was in the Temple speaking to the wise men until then? Historians have many theories, some of which must be considered.

What was happening in Palestine?

The Jews were under submission to the Roman Empire and were governed by puppet figures. The country had been divided into two since the year 6 AD: Galilee, where Herod Antipas ruled, and Judea, which was administered by a Roman ombudsman. A people under submission are seldom at peace, at least behind closed doors.

There were different sects, such as the Sadducees, who were rich landowners that worked with the Romans. Many of their members were part of the priestly aristocracy. They were conservative and denied any doctrine that was not confirmed by the Scriptures, for example, the resurrection of the dead and the sufferings of hell.

There were also the Pharisees, which are not 'fairly' reflected in the Gospels as they permanently opposed anything Roman, though normally their resistance was passive. They can be considered the strictest theologians of the time; they believed in resurrection and immortality, but they took the oral interpretation of the Law of Moses as a dogma.

And the Essenians are taken by many historians to have inspired the ideas that Jesus preached. The members of this sect lived in poverty, were mystically oriented and lived in the desert "preparing the way of the Lord, making straight his path." They lived in groups under a singular, strict form of discipline, preparing for the end times in which the kingdom of God would arrive under the authority of the Messiah. They were organised into a sort of 'salvation army', and promoted the idea of the holy war.

The Essenians always walked in pairs

The Essenians were commanded by their 'twelve best' members, taking the number of tribes in ancient Israel. Their religious ceremony consisted of a 'community banquet', very similar to the last supper of Christ and his disciples: "a holy man held out his hand to invoke blessing, taking bread and wine, around a long table where other brothers were seated."

Did Christ learn from the Essenians?

The Essenians believed themselves to be the renovators of the Alliance and experienced it as a foretaste of the kingdom to come. To become a part of their sect, one had to sever all ties with the past, even family, in order to begin a training process. All new arrivals were baptised as a sign of penitence, but, unlike the Christians, this water ritual was repeated at regular intervals to get rid of any evil thoughts or intentions.

All Essenians had to be good in both thought and deed. The elders examined the consciences of the youngest among them and were examined by others the same age as them. Liars, robbers, violent people and those harbouring resentment and vengeance, received the severest punishment. When one of the members of the sect was caught doing something wrong, he was reprimanded in private; if he sinned again, he was punished before witnesses, and if he repeated the offence, he was punished in public. The judges' maxim was, "correct others with love and humility, and never forget that you are dealing with your brother."

The Essenians believed they were following a path and considered themselves 'the society of many'. Nobody had any possessions, and everything was shared by the community. They practised 'holy poverty' as a way of life. We could cite many more examples to show that the evangelists Matthew and John must have been strongly influenced by Essenian texts when they wrote their own. The theology of this sect can be summed up as follows (extract from their *Manual of Discipline*):

From the God of knowledge comes the existence of everything that is and will be... He created man so that he might dominate the world and gave him two spirits in which to walk until the time of his coming. These are the spirits of truth and perversion. All men are sons of light under the reign of the prince of light or sons of darkness under the reign of the angel of darkness. Life in our time is the battlefield between these spirits, and all the spirits under the command of the angel of darkness, or the spirit of perversion, are working to make the sons of light fall. The place where the two spirits fight is the inner heart of man... For God has made them equal until the creation of the new is declared, so that mankind may know good and evil.

This type of duality appears in the writings of Saint Paul and many passages of the New Testament. It can also be found in the teachings of John the Baptist, yet it is in his messages that we can really appreciate their influence. In Jesus' message it is less clear, although it is obvious that he was influenced to some extent by them.

The Zealots

The Zealots were not considered a sect, though they were made up of people who had belonged to the Philistines and the Essenians among other groups. We know that in the year 6 AD, when Rome made the decision to directly control Judea, a rabbi of Pharisee origin known as Judas of Galilee, formed a sort of violent revolutionary movement. When Jesus was at his most active, they were playing a very important role in Palestine.

They continued working after the Crucifixion and sparked an armed revolt in 66 AD. This was repressed in four years and cost nearly 20,000 Jews their lives, caused great devastation in Jerusalem and the plundering of the temple. But the last Zealots took refuge in the armed fortress of Masada where they spent nearly three years in the company of other compatriots of different sects and social groups.

The flames of the Zealot movement did not die out and another rebellion broke out in 132, which was lost three years later. Then, the emperor Hadrian decreed the expulsion of all the Jews from Judea, and Jerusalem passed into Roman hands, being renamed Aelia Capitolina.

The eighteen years of silence

The passage of the Scriptures where Jesus is with the Wise Men in the temple at twelve years of age makes it obvious that he was preoccupied with religious and social concerns. Even though we are told he was under his family's charge, we do not believe that this was so for the next eighteen years. He had enough time to travel through all the countries in the area, to get to Egypt and even to India. There is a great deal of literature on the 'secret activities of the young Jesus' which has him among the pyramids of the Nile drawing the inside of them onto the sand, including their astronomers' observatories, even though only priests were allowed inside them. No foreigners were ever allowed to see the maps of the pyramids.

It is also said that he reached the Indo valley to learn about the local religions and medicinal practices. Fida Hassnain, in his book *The Other Story of Jesus*, says that he might have come into contact with the doctrine of Varadhamana Mahavira (599-527 BC), who preached the purification of the spirit through the ascetic life, non-violence, kindness of spirit and action, respect for all living things, including a vegetarian diet. The *Jain*, Mahavira's sect, may have begged him to stay with them, but he decided to continue along his way to the temple of Jagannath of Puri, in Orissa.

He stayed there for about six years, wanting to visit certain cities that were held sacred by the Hindus, particularly those along the shores of the Ganges. In this way he was able to learn of the Vedic religion and customs. Later, Jesus came into contact with the Buddhists of Nepal, where he was taken in as a brother. He investigated this religion thoroughly and we have no doubt that he soaked himself in the Sutras, the Vinayas and the Abhidarma, and that this allowed him to acquire the skill of preaching, so much so that he was compared to Buddha himself.

Is this somewhat fantastical? There are documents that prove it so, although their authenticity has not been demonstrated. However, his eighteen years of silence mean that these and other more daring theories can be considered – such as the one that tells of Jesus in Egypt, meeting the Essenians once again. The elders greeted him with great jubilation and after hearing him for a short while, had to admit that he was wiser and more prudent. Nor were they were not surprised to find that he was aiming higher, though he would go through testing times.

One such trial would bring him immortality and above all the confirmation of his name: Jesus, a symbol of sincerity, faith and philanthropy. The future Saviour of humankind spent forty days in a monastery immersed in deep meditation.

When this time was over, he had dominated himself and could speak more naturally. Then, he was given a parchment on which only the word 'heroism' was written. With this, he was given the idea that he was going to go through the greatest of tribulations and would get through them with an entirety of spirit superior to that of most mortals, because he was the

Christ. For this reason, whenever the Essenians of Egypt came across him, they repeated the same message: "Amen". He had become immortal.

Of course, what we have just presented is yet another hypothesis, backed up by Levi, one of the greatest experts on the 'secret life' of Jesus. Its inclusion here is designed to give an idea of what can happen when part of such an important person's existence is silenced.

Something else worth pointing out is that Jesus was oriental by birth and spent these years of his 'training' in a very different environment to Greece and Rome, the two cradles of Western thought. So we should see him from a very different perspective to our traditions.

Neither should it be forgotten that Jesus was a Man, not at all a 'superman' with extraordinary powers. Just as Yahweh had allowed the Universe, the Earth and everything living to evolve in its own time instead of creating it as we know it, he allowed his son to grow at his own speed. And he did so in the spirit of the knowledge to be found in those hard lands.

When this Man pricked himself he felt pain; he got tired on long walks, felt hungry two or three times a day, needed to drink as often as us, and was at the mercy of all human weaknesses. Only his intelligence and capacity for suffering and the security his destiny proffered gave him the strength of will to keep him on the straight and narrow. But nobody doubts that he made mistakes at certain times in his life, although he was always careful to rectify things afterwards, except in the selection of his disciples and at other important times.

CHAPTER IV

JESUS CHRIST AND JOHN THE BAPTIST

The versions of Matthew and Luke

In the Gospel according to Matthew (3:1-12) the following version is given:

In those days came John the Baptist, preaching in the wilderness of Judea, "Repent, for the kingdom of heaven is at hand." For this is he who was spoken of by the prophet Isaiah when he said,

"The voice of one crying in the wilderness: Prepare the way of the Lord, make his paths straight."

Now John wore a garment of camel's hair, and a leather girdle around his waist; and his food was locusts and wild honey. They went out to him Jerusalem and all Judea and all the region about the Jordan, and they were baptized by him in the river Jordan, confessing their sins.

But when he saw many of the Pharisees and Sadducees coming for baptism, he said to them, "You brood of vipers! Who warned you to flee form the wrath to come? Bear fruit that befits repentance, and do not presume to say to yourselves, 'We have Abraham as our father'; for I tell you, God is able from these stones to raise up children to Abraham. Even now the axe is laid to the root of the trees; every three therefore that does not bear good fruit is cut down and thrown into the fire.

"I baptize you with water for repentance, but he who is coming after me is mightier than I, whose sandals I am not

49

worth to carry; he will baptize you with the Holy Spirit and with fire. His winnowing fork is in his hand, and he will clear his threshing floor and gather his wheat into the granary, but the chaff he will burn with unquenchable fire."

This is complemented by Luke's version. After summing up the activities of John the Baptist, he adds (Luke 3:10-20):

And the multitudes asked him, "What then shall we do?" And he answered them, "He who has two coats, let him share with him who has none; and he who has food, let him do like-wise." Tax collectors also came to be baptized, and said to him, "Teacher, what shall we do?" And he said to them, "Collect no more than is appointed you." Soldiers also asked him, "And we, what shall we do?" And he said to them, "Rob no one by violence or by false accusation, and be content with your wages."

As the people were in expectation, and all men questioned in their hearts concerning John, whether perhaps he were the Christ, John answered them all, "I baptize you with water; but he who is mightier than I is coming, the thong of whose sandals I am not worthy to untie; he will baptize you with the Holy Spirit and with fire. His winnowing fork is in his hand, to clear his threshing floor, and to gather his wheat into his granary, but the chaff he will burn with unquenchable fire."

So, with many other exhortations, he preached good news to the people. But Herod the tetrarch, who had been reproved by him for Herodias, his brother's wife, and for all the evil things that Herod had done, added this to them all, that he shut up John in prison.

Who was John the Baptist really?

Little is known about John the Baptist. The only informa-tion we have is that he was the son of the priest Zechariah and Elizabeth, who conceived him miraculously. Elizabeth was Mary's first cousin, and the two told each other their secrets. This is how we know that an angel appeared to Zechariah to announce to him:

The baptisms by John

Do not be afraid, Zechariah, for your prayer is heard, and your wife Elizabeth will bear you a son, and you shall call his name John. And you will have joy and gladness, and many will rejoice at his birth; for he will be great before the Lord, and he shall drink no wine nor strong drink, and he will be filled with the Holy Spirit, even from his mother's womb.

It is written that as soon as he was born, John gave glory to God, amazing all present as they had never seen a baby that could talk as soon as it came out of its mother's womb. This behaviour is similar to the legends on reincarnated lamas or 'tulkus' that can begin to speak, and on occasions preach, as soon as they are born.

Some researchers believe that both John and Jesus belonged to the order of the Essenians of Jutha, who lived near the mountain of Massada. John learnt the better part of his doctrine alongside these mystical people. Finally, he went to live in the desert until the moment came to be seen and heard by Israel.

Preparing the way of the lord

Soon John the Baptist began to show that his main mission was to prepare the way of Jesus. This can be seen in the Gospel of John (1:15-34)

John bore witness to him, and cried, "This was he of whom I said, 'He who comes after me ranks before me, for he was before me.'" And from his fullness have we all received, grace upon grace. For the law was given through Moses; grace and truth came through Jesus Christ. No one has ever seen God; the only Son, who is in the bosom of the Father, he has made him known.

And this is the testimony of John, when the Jews sent priests and Levites from Jerusalem to ask him, "Who are you?" He confessed, he did not deny, but confessed, "I am not the Christ." And they asked him, "What then? Are you Elijah?" He said, "I am not." "Are you the prophet?" And he answered, "No." They said to him then, "Who are you? Let us have an answer for those who sent us. What do you say about yourself?" He said, "I am the voice of one crying out in the wilderness, 'Make straight the way of the Lord,' as the prophet Isaiah said."

Now they had been sent from the Pharisees. They asked him, "Then why are you baptizing, if you are neither the Christ, nor Elijah, nor the prophet?" John answered them, "I baptize with water; but among you stands one whom you do not know, even he who comes after me, the thong of whose sandal I am not worth to untie." This took place in Bethany beyond the Jordan, where John was baptizing.

The next day he saw Jesus coming toward him and said, "Behold, the Lamb of God, who takes away the sin of the world! This is he of whom I said, 'After me comes a man who ranks before me, for he was before me.' I myself did not know him; but for this I came baptizing with water, that he might be revealed to Israel." And John bore witness, "I saw the Spirit descend as a dove from heaven, and it remained on him. I myself did not know him; but he who sent me to baptize with water said to me, 'He on whom you see the Spirit descend and remain, this is he who baptizes with the Holy Spirit.' And I have seen and have borne witness that this is the Son of God."

The Gospel of John is one of the clearest proofs of the function of John the Baptist as the man who introduced Jesus, but it is strange that only a small mention is made of his baptism. Still, there is no doubt that he considered him to be the

Son of God, "whom he did not know". They could not meet while they were with the Essenians, if they ever actually were.

The Gospel of John is the most hermetic of them all and its messages require a serene interpretation. It is said to have been written for more highly educated people.

The baptism by John

'To baptise' comes from the Greek word *baptizein*, meaning 'to submerge in water'. John carried out baptisms as a way of washing the sins of those who wished to undertake a process of spiritual regeneration. To do so they first had to make a confession. This was not a very common process among the Jews, however, although they had started to use it as a way of cleansing themselves of the "impurities of exile or contagion from pagan practices." The Essenians of the Qumran practised it regularly. John gave it a more solemn, final air by making it the only entrance for those who awaited the arrival of the Messiah.

Isaac Asimov believes that John the Baptist used the waters of the River Jordan when he remembered the advice that Elijah gave to Naman the leper:

Go and cleanse yourself in the Jordan and you will be pure.

Among the Israelis, circumcision was the sacred initiation rite that allowed their children to enter into religious life. But Christians preferred baptism, as it served as a reminder of the gospels. In Matthew (3:13-17) this is explained as follows:

Then Jesus came from Galilee to the Jordan to John, to be baptized by him. John would have prevented him, saying, "I need to be baptized by you, and do you come to me?" But Jesus answered him, "Let it be so now; for thus it is fitting for us to fulfil all righteousness." Then he consented. And when Jesus was baptized, he went up immediately from the water, and behold, the heavens were opened and he saw the

Spirit of God descending like a dove, and alighting on him; and lo, a voice from heaven, saying, "This is my beloved Son, with whom I am well pleased."

The baptism of Jesus (drawing by Rembrandt)

In the passage from Luke (3:21-22), we can read:

Now when all the people were baptized, and when Jesus also had been baptized and was praying, the heaven was opened, and the Holy Spirit descended upon him in bodily form, as a dove, and voice came from heaven, "Thou art my beloved Son; with thee I am well pleased."

In the Gospel according to Mark, Jesus' baptism is very similar to the previous ones. What is surprising is the brevity of the reference that Luke makes of it, in comparison to Matthew who talks of it more extensively and, particularly, stresses the condition of John the Baptist as Jesus' precursor, although Jesus is a far superior being.

The moment that is narrated should be considered extremely important, as it is the forerunner to three years of intense public activity by Jesus, ending in the crucifixion and days later with the Resurrection. Historians do not agree on how old Jesus was: some say he had reached 29 or 30, while others have him down as being 33.

In the Gospel according to John (3:22-36) a new testimony is offered by John the Baptist:

After this Jesus and his disciples went into the land of Judea; there he remained with them and baptized. John also was baptizing at Aenon near Salim, because there was much water there; and people came and were baptized. For John had not yet been put in prison.

Now a discussion arose between John's disciples and a Jew over purifying. And they came to John, and said to him, "Rabbi, he who was with you beyond the Jordan, to whom you bore witness, here he is, baptizing, and all are going to him." John answered, "No one can receive anything except what is given him from heaven. You yourselves bear me witness, that I said, I am not the Christ, but I have been sent before him. He who has the bride is the bridegroom; the friend of the bridegroom, who stands and hears him, rejoices greatly at the bridegroom's voice; therefore this joy of mine is now full. He must increase, but I must decrease."

He who comes from above is above all; he who is of the earth belongs to the earth, and of the earth he speaks; he who comes from heaven is above all. He bears witness to what he has seen and heard, yet no one receives his testimony; he who receives his testimony sets his seal to this, that God is true. For he whom God has sent utters the words of God, for it is not by measure that he gives the Spirit; the Father loves the Son, and has given all things into his hand. He who believes in the Son has eternal life; he who does not obey the Son shall not see life, but the wrath of God rests upon him.

The words of John the Baptist take on prophetic proportions – he could hardly have been understood by those who heard him. It was necessary to write them down to be able to analyse them carefully. Luke quoted them so that this could be done, without worrying too much if they were too hermetic.

However, the allusions that John makes to Jesus as Messiah do not fit in with Matthew's version, as he ended up proving that John the Baptist did not know of the true mission of Jesus. This is a frequent contradiction in the Gospels, solved by the theologians by declaring that "sacred texts can never be interpreted literally." The truth is that we inevitably do so, especially when we want to understand them individually.

Jesus becomes aware of his destiny

Jesus had actually been performing baptisms, but probably not on a large scale, for a very long time. He had followed in John the Baptist's footsteps, until he became aware of his destiny. He had to preach a revolutionary doctrine, almost a compendium of many others known at the time in the Orient, with the exception that he used the most direct example. This was implicit in the words of his Father: "This is my beloved Son, with whom I am well pleased."

This implied taking on a divine role within the body of a man. Jesus felt the weight of his responsibility, and doubted. He did not believe himself ready. He left everything and went to the desert to seek refuge, meditate and discover his strength.

CHAPTER V

AFTER TEMPTATION

The most absolute solitude

Jesus had never been alone. Since his birth in the cavern-like stable he had always been with someone. The few times he had tried to seek solitude had been to analyse what he had come across. After his baptism by John he was confronted by two situations in a hostile terrain where the difference in temperature between night and day could be as much as thirty degrees. This was the desert, where he was "led by the Spirit" (the Gospel according to Saint Mark).

Water was scarce, as was food, with the only edible things being wild fruit and the leaves of certain plants. He is thought to have spent forty days on the barren mountain of Yebel Qarantal, one of the most desolate areas of the Judean desert.

He might have acted like a Buddhist ascetic, reaching such a level of mental concentration that he would not have needed food or drink for several days. He also went into a low level of mental activity but did not lose consciousness. Meanwhile, the lizards around him, the flies that buzzed, the heat and the cold were telling him that God had created absolutely everything with a logical function in mind.

Time seemed to have stopped, with no sounds other than those of nature, the stones moving or the cracking of the earth burnt by the sun. These were certainly not ideal conditions for Jesus to reflect on his destiny. He did not know how things would develop, but a cold sweat foretold something.

Later on, around the end of the fifth week while he slowly chewed some leaves next to a well he had just dug with his bare hands, in whose depths an underground spring flowed, he felt strong and analysed the words that John had said to him on the shores of the Jordan:

...This is he of whom I said, 'After me comes a man who ranks before me, for he was before me.' I myself did not know him; but for this I came baptizing with water, that he might be revealed to Israel.

He had to 'appear' before his people, leave his family and his previous life and live a very different life from that of the Baptist. He did not fully agree with John's apocalyptic message either, preferring to preach goodness and love and raise people's spirits. Through grace, never fear, men and women could be converted.

Am I truly the Chosen One?

Jesus slowly became aware of his condition as a Man who had to set an example for all human beings. His mind filled with images, words and facts that he had never seen nor heard until then; projections of the near future. He was not afraid, but he saw his enemies there.

Soon, one question formed in his mind above all others: "Am I truly the Chosen One?" Everything pointed to an affirmative answer, but modesty stopped him from admitting it, until a voice came from somewhere outside him, perhaps someone hiding in the rocks nearby, saying,

"If you are the Son of God, command these stones to become loaves of bread."

Jesus' mind grew firm, his mouth filled with saliva and his voice came out clearly:

"Man shall not live by bread alone, but by every word that proceeds from the mouth of God."

Jesus praying in the desert (drawing by Rembrandt)

He had shot these verbal darts at Satan, his omnipresent enemy. At other times he had felt him to be close, but he had never dared to challenge him so brazenly.

Tempting one who had never experienced greed

Suddenly Jesus found himself on the cupola of the Temple of Jerusalem. Below his feet the other buildings seemed like miniatures and the floor was far away. Jesus felt vertigo and this was an ideal opening for the enemy to come back with his temptations.

"If you are the Son of God, throw yourself down; for it is written, 'He will give his angels charge of you,' and 'On their hands they will bear you up, lest you strike your foot against a stone.'"

With this invitation, the roofs turned to gold and the people in the streets clamoured for more: the best way for him to be received among them. But Jesus did not know vanity, and gave this strong answer:

"Again it is written, 'You shall not tempt the Lord your God.'"

It was a direct confrontation between Good and Evil. Jesus must have felt extremely weak after his forty days' fasting, and Satan thought he would be able to bend his will. It was just a matter of insisting, of surrounding the solitary man with seductive illusions.

He still thought magic was his best weapon. All he had to do was to place an irresistible temptation before Jesus, for example by taking him to the top of a mountain and letting him see all the kingdoms in the world spread out at his feet: a mass of riches, glitter and seductive colours. The best thing to support his inviting words:

"All these I will give you, if you will fall down and worship me."

Jesus immediately replied as violently as if he had stepped on the head of a poisonous snake:

"Be gone, Satan! For it is written, 'You shall worship the Lord your God, and him only shall you serve.'"

And the enemy fled in defeat and left only the hollow of his voice. The man who did not know what coveting was stood staring at the wide desert, a beautiful, though desolate place, and decided to leave. He knew now what awaited him, but was sure he would be able to face it. He had no doubt at all that he was the Chosen One.

The imprisonment of John the Baptist

Although Jesus had accepted his fate, he still felt insecure at times. He had certain doubts he wished to clear up. A few hours after he set off, after washing and eating some berries and shoots, he went to the River Jordan. He wanted to speak to John, perhaps to try to convince him not to be so aggressive in his diatribes against the Pharisees and governors.

When he saw a large crowd on the right shore of the river, his intentions vanished. He could see that the people there were stirring in agitation and as he got closer was able to hear angry voices. Then he saw a group of soldiers on the other side of the group brandishing their swords and daggers. This made him very uneasy.

"What has happened?" he asked one of the calmer members of the group.

"Where have you been, stranger, that you have not heard what has happened this morning?" shouted the man in surprise. He was wearing the clothes of a shoemaker. "Herod Antipas has put John the Baptist into prison! By now he must be inside a dungeon no-one has ever managed to get out of!"

The news was like a blow to the stomach for Jesus. He took it silently, with a shiver. He stood still as the other man walked away swearing and said to himself that these were not times for violent sermons. He was sorry for the suffering John must be going through and he understood that his desire for justice must have led him to insult those in power. It was not the first time that a prophet had done this without caring about the possible bloody consequences.

The first disciples

Jesus left the Jordan with Andrew and John, two of the Baptist's followers, by his side. A few months previously they had expressed their desire to follow the future Messiah and in his absence had wondered if they would ever see him again, so they were very happy to see him.

They only had to hear him pronounce a few sentences to be filled with enthusiasm and hope at his openness of speech, which needed no interpretation. Andrew went to look for his brother Peter and said to him:

"I have found a Master worth following. What he says is crystal clear and pure."

John also went to find his brother James, and thus different men came to be by Jesus' side. Jesus himself then went to Bethsaida to find Phillip, who was very shy. He invited him to be his 'follower' and this alone was enough for him to abandon everything else and join him.

After a few days Phillip felt secure enough in his new situation to call the shepherd Nathaniel and say to him:

"We have found him of whom Moses in the law and also the prophets wrote, Jesus of Nazareth, the son of Joseph."

"Can anything good come out of Nazareth?" asked Nathaniel, thinking of the unfair reputation the town had.

"Come and see."

The shepherd was not fully convinced, but went to see Jesus nevertheless and was greeted thus:

"Behold, an Israelite indeed, in whom is no guile!"

"How do you know me?" asked Nathaniel, surprised.

"Before Philip called you, when you were under the fig tree, I saw you."

"Rabbi, you are the Son of God! You are the King of Israel!"

Jesus at the weddings in Cana

"Because I say to you, I saw you under the fig tree, do you believe?" said Jesus in his sure, sincere voice. "You shall see greater things than these."

"He looked at his first disciples and continued, "Truly, truly, I say to you, you will see heaven opened, and the angel of God ascending and descending upon the Son of man."

65

Shortly afterwards Jesus and his first disciples left the Jordan valley to travel to Galilee.

The weddings at Cana

When the group got to Cana they were met by jubilant music and people dressed in colourful clothing. They were soon surrounded by dancers, some of them so dizzy they seemed drunk.

Jesus recognised some of his cousins and realised he had not been invited to the wedding because he had left home in search of his destiny. When the dancers went up to him they asked him how he felt after his baptism in the Jordan, how long he had spent in the desert, and who his followers were.

Jesus did not answer as the first thing he wanted to do was to go to his mother, whom he could see in the garden. He went up to her, kissed her forehead and took her hands in his. Mary had felt very lonely over the last few weeks. She was a mother like any other, even though she had given birth to the Son of God. Over the last twenty-nine years she had often had to say goodbye to him for many months. But this time, a painful foreboding was telling her that this was now the 'point of no return.'

Perhaps to rid herself of the bitter ideas in her head, Mary forced a smile and looked at her son, whose hands still held her with a comforting heat. He knew he was about to hear a request from her:

"The owners of this house have run out of wine."

Mary must have known that her son had not broken his family ties for these minor matters, but the spirit of domesticity was more important to her at this moment. The wedding ceremony would end halfway through the afternoon if the wine ran out. This would mean failure for the hosts, as the guests were not supposed to leave until the next day. They had to find a way to keep them there.

"O woman, what have you to do with me?" asked Jesus, with a reproach similar to the one he had made in the temple so many years ago, when his parents had thought him to be lost. He added, "My hour has not yet come."

Tears came to the woman's eyes for the mistake she had made. She never again intervened in her son's affairs and almost asked him for forgiveness. Jesus, however, asked the servants to bring him the six empty earthenware jars. When they were in front of him he asked for them to be filled with water. Then he said:

"Draw some water from the jar, and take it to the steward of the feast."

The steward took a sip of this 'water' and was so shocked that he ran to find the bridegroom. He almost shouted in his disgust:

"Every man serves the good wine first; and when men have drunk freely, then the poor wine; but you have kept the good wine until now."

"But... what are you saying?" the groom stuttered, looking at Jesus.

Then they realised that the six jars no longer held water, but wine, the most delicious wine that had ever been tasted in Cana. Mary and Jesus' disciples and family knew that they had beheld a miracle.

But there were others who considered the prodigy an act of magic, another of the acts of miracle-workers who sometimes appeared, and whose artifices were told of all over Israel. These were lands where amazing acts were common, and many of them were tricks or collective fantasies.

We now know that Jesus had worked a true miracle. He actually knew his countrymen better than anyone, and was prepared to meet incomprehension and insults, because what he proposed would be seen as a revolution, especially by his enemies.

The Message is heard at Capernaum

Jesus and his disciples went to Capernaum, where many of them lived. It was easier to instruct them in a new doctrine without them having to leave their homes and usual occupations. It was also one of the largest towns in the region and a stopping off place for caravans on their way to Damascus from the ports on the Sea of Galilee. Wise men, scribes and traders all met there and most of them frequented the synagogues.

In those times it was common for outsiders to read passages from the sacred book aloud and then comment on them. When Jesus did so, the hundreds of men inside the temple forgot even their own thoughts – they were captivated by the power of his speech!

When they heard him they forgot even the passing of time in the clarity and ease of understanding of his readings and comments. Nobody needed to know the sacred texts firsthand, the terminology of the rabbi or the winding discourse of the Pharisees. His words were exact and he used common, human parables with an emotional message that went straight to their hearts. And he forewarned them by announcing:

"These times are coming to their end, and soon the kingdom of heaven will be among you! Repent and prepare yourself for the good news!"

Then, those present asked themselves, "Who is this man who speaks with such a sweet voice? Where has he learnt such emotive, sincere speech? How can he be a wise man if he wears such different clothes to the masters'?"

And this was true – Jesus did not wear the four-fringed cape that the law required of teachers. Someone suddenly said that they had seen him on the shores of the Jordan, but nobody believed this as John's followers apparently never left the river, and Jesus had not asked them to be baptised.

Jesus speaking at the Temple

The fishermen and peasants were the first who wished to follow Jesus, hearing him compare the kingdom of heaven with a net that catches both good and bad fish. And he gave them the image of a great field, where seeds are scattered in the furrows for it to take root, or on the edges of pathways where it will be left to the mercy of the hoe or birds.

Nobody had ever given them such practical examples and those who heard them elbowed each other and felt totally united with the preacher. Further on, when they heard him speak in the streets, nobody was surprised to see women leaving their household chores when he compared sinners to an old tunic that becomes impossible to mend, or contaminated recipients, which should never be used to hold new wine. And they perfectly understood the parable of the housewife who turns her house upside down to search for the missing denarius, or a widow who was unjustly treated by the judges.

CHAPTER VI

IN THE HEART OF A SOCIETY THAT NEEDED TO BELIEVE

A blow to the merchants

Jesus had just turned thirty when he got ready to celebrate the Passover in the temple of Jerusalem. As soon as he went up the first steps of the great staircase, the disciples saw a sudden change come over him: his face hardened, his entire body became tensed like a bow ready to shoot, and his hands were like a hunter's about to deal with his prey.

Before him were the traders doing their business and advertising their wares with shouts and insults to those who refused to pay their high prices. They were sacrificing animals whose cries filled the air and whose blood stained everything around. It was a repulsive scene that had been going on for over forty years, and the priests were so cynical that trade was carried out in the most sacred areas of the temple.

Jesus came in like a whirlwind, so violently that hundreds of merchants and buyers, men and women, had to escape to avoid ending up in the same condition as the overturned stalls, tables, chairs, cages and other things. They did not even bother to pick up the coins that had fallen. Meanwhile, they heard:

"Take these things away; you shall not make my Father's house a house of trade!"

Some of the people there remembered the prophecy about the Son of God: "Zeal for thy house will consume me." When they saw that Jesus was calmer, they asked him:

"What sign have you to show us for doing this?"

Destroy this temple, and in three days I will raise it up."

His listeners thought he was referring to the physical part of the building. They were incredulous:

"It has taken forty-six years to build this temple, and will you raise it up in three days?"

The disciples were the only ones who understood some time later that the Master was referring to the temple each believer carries within him.

The verbal attack of the possessed man

Over the next few weeks, Jesus continued to preach and had some strange experiences with it. One morning while he was speaking to a crowd in a square, one man fell to the ground and went into terrible convulsions. His mouth frothed and he said from his throat:

"Ah! What have you to do with us, Jesus of Nazareth? Have you come to destroy us? I know who you are, the Holy One of God."

Jesus understood that his enemies had brought this unhappy creature to him, a possessed man who was repeating what others made him learn. It was quite an efficient weapon with men, as the silence of the crowd proved. Some of them looked at him in distrust, when before they had listened to him in admiration when he came among them. Jesus knelt before the fallen man, lifted him up by his shoulders and looked at him. Then he ordered, with a voice that echoed in the surrounding walls:

"Be silent, and come out of him!"

The possessed man writhed with the combat that was being staged inside him by the devil wanting to escape from inside his prey. A while later he was calmer, and soon managed to stand up, pale and exhausted, seeming to be cured, though he could remember nothing of what had happened.

Jesus throwing the traders out of the temple

Once again, some of the crowd said that they had been watching a magician who could get rid of devils like the prophets of old times. But even more of them thought that what had happened was another miracle and should be spoken about all over Palestine.

An image of the world of poverty

Nicodemus, one of the rabbis who made up the Sanhedrin (the Jewish Supreme Court) had seen the possessed man being cured. He was a wise man and was well aware that what he had seen was no magic act. He straightaway decided that he must meet Jesus.

But he did not want to do so openly because he was afraid to put his job at risk. He knew what had happened to John the Baptist, who was still in the dungeons of Herod Antipas' palace. Jan Dobraczynski, a Polish novelist who dared to tell the story of the man from Nazareth through Nicodemus' voice, gives us a very clear insight into the man's attitude as well as the environment Jesus lived in:

It was nighttime when I left my house. I was wrapped in a black simlah. *The round moon bathed the town in a tenuous light. Occasionally everything went black when the clouds covered it, but the blackness was very short and the wind strong. I was accompanied by two of my most faithful servants. We descended the stairs and entered the black depths of the lower city. Above our heads stretched the arcades of the aqueduct. We left the elegant zone of the palaces and came, as if to the edge of a cliff, to the dark anthill of the cave dwellings. I never would have suspected that in Jerusalem itself, so close to the temple, such a mass of dwellings could exist, in which water and earth ran into the waste. Judas went before us, clearing the way skilfully and quickly over the remains. I realised he knew the place like the back of his hand. In the twilight the miserable buildings seemed to be heaped onto each other like desperate men climbing a mountain of corpses. My uneasiness grew as we went into the maze, a place I don't think I could have got out of by my own means.*

This image gives some idea of the places Jesus frequented. The iconography of the Gospels, that is, the illustrations or photograms they are portrayed in, give us an idea of clean people in an almost idyllic environment, where even the bad people are well dressed. This is all false. The poor people lived in wretched homes and were dirty and their clothing torn and patched. There were no drains and no one bothered to clean the streets, except those where the powerful people went. Bad nutrition was evident in the hundreds of sick or decrepit people, in the poor and in the enormous social inequalities of the time. They also smelt bad, though this might not be so important, as they were used to it.

Remembering this will help us to understand why Jesus moved the poor of Israel so. Nobody had ever spoken to them directly to tell them that "they were nearer to the kingdom of God than the rich," or that "all men are equal in the eyes of God, though he always favours the humble."

Jesus gains a strong ally

To continue with the story of Nicodemus, he eventually managed to meet up with Jesus. They did so clandestinely and their meeting began as follows:

"No one can do these signs that you do, unless God is with him."

"Truly, truly, I say to you, unless one is born anew, he cannot see the kingdom of God."

These words were intentionally hermetic but Nicodemus understood them.

"How can a man be born when he is old? Can he enter a second time into his mother's womb and be born?"

"That which is born of the flesh is flesh, and that which is born of the Spirit is spirit. Do not marvel that I said to you, 'You must be born anew.'" Jesus paused, lifted his right hand and continued. "The wind blows where it wills, and you hear the sound of it, but you do not know whence it comes or whither it goes; so it is with every one who is born of the Spirit."

Nicodemus was disconcerted. The word games were difficult to comprehend and he inquired again:

"How can this be?"

"Are you a teacher of Israel, and yet you do not understand this? Truly, truly, I say to you, we speak of what we know, and bear witness to what we have seen; but you do not receive our testimony. If I have told you earthly things and you do not believe, how can you believe if I tell you heavenly things? No one has ascended into heaven but he who descended from heaven, the Son of Man."

Then Nicodemus began to believe in Jesus, because he understood his words; he was being invited to regenerate himself, to transform all his moral concepts. But more surprises awaited him:

"And as Moses lifted up the serpent in the wilderness, so must the Son of man be lifted up, that whoever believes in him may have eternal life."

When the important member of the Sanhedrin left the house, he had become one of Jesus' most important allies. But he did not change his life. He carried on in the same position. We now know that through his intervention, Jesus did not die sooner. Nicodemus also challenged the judges to save the crucified man's body.

This made him one of the main members of the Christian community. He is said to have written an apocryphal gospel, used by Grégoire de Tours, and to have introduced the legend of the Holy Grail.

Feeding the five thousand

Jesus was followed by a large crowd in Jerusalem. These were times of pilgrimages that brought thousands of people to the holy city of the Jews. The desire of most of them to follow the man from Nazareth was apparently a little too strong for the priests' liking.

They did not even leave him alone when he went up a mountain. They had been by his side a long time and some of the disciples remembered that it was lunchtime and that the people must be hungry. The best idea was to send them off in search of food. But Jesus did not share this idea. He said:

"You give them something to eat."

"We have only five loaves here and two fish," said one of the disciples. "There must be more than five thousand people here, men, women and children."

"Separate them into groups of fifty," requested the Master. "I will do the rest."

Then he took the five loaves and two fish, raised his eyes to heaven, blessed them and handed them to his disciples so that they could share them out among the crowd. There was food for all, and even twelve baskets left over.

This miracle made Jesus one of the most famous 'magicians' of Jerusalem. Few of them saw him as the Messiah or the Son of God. And even fewer were able to understand the mystery of the Eucharist that had just commenced.

Walking on water

The next day, Jesus told his disciples to take a boat and wait for him on the other side of the lake. He wanted to say goodbye to the crowds that still waited for him. With his most beautiful words he fulfilled this brotherly requirement and then went up the mountain to pray on it's the summit. He was alone.

Night fell and a fierce storm brought him out of his contemplative state, or perhaps he realised that something dangerous was happening. Sure enough, in the middle of the lake, the boat his disciples were in was being thrown about by large waves. The strong wind ripped the sails and took away the oars, and the crew faced drowning and death.

It was three in the morning when the elements calmed, though clouds still darkened the sky. A dense blackness enveloped the broken boat, whose occupants had no idea how they were still alive. Suddenly one of them saw a figure. It seemed like a tall man, but they thought it was a ghost.

"Do not fear," said Jesus. "It is I." He was walking on water.

"Lord, if it is you, bring me to you," asked Peter.

"Come by my side."

The apostle got out of the boat, but was unexpectedly buffeted by the wind and began to be afraid. When this happened he began to sink. He was terrified and shouted, "Lord, save me!"

Jesus' hand came to his aid and he scolded him kindly:

"Man of little faith, why did you doubt?"

As soon as they got into the boat the wind died down. All the men in the boat knelt down to adore their Master, and exclaimed,

"Truly you are the Son of God!"

They continued sailing until they got to Genesaret, where there were many people waiting who had heard of Jesus. They came with the sick members of their family, and all were cured. Some of them only had to touch Christ's robes to be healed.

Jesus saving Peter while he walks on water

The encounter with the Samaritan

Jesus and his disciples returned to Galilee. They were very tired from their travels through Samaria and needed a rest. They were near a well quite close to the town of Sicas. They knew that this well had been dug by Jacob himself centuries before.

A few minutes later, when his disciples had gone to find food and water, Jesus went up to a Samaritan, who was drawing a bucket of water and said to her:

"Give me a drink."

The woman looked at him, surprised, because nobody had spoken so naturally to her for a long time. She had had five husbands and lived as a concubine, and was one of an inferior tribe. So she asked:

"How is it that you, a Jew, ask a drink of me, a woman of Samaria?

"If you knew the gift of God and who it is that is saying to you, 'Give me a drink,' you would have asked him, and he would have given you living water," replied Jesus with a smile.

"Sir, you have nothing to draw with, and the well is deep; where do you get that living water? Are you greater than our father Jacob, who gave us the well, and drank from it himself, and his sons, and his cattle?"

"Every one who drinks of this water will thirst again, but whoever drinks of the water that I shall give him will never thirst; the water that I shall give him will become in him a spring of water welling up into eternal life."

"Sir, give me this water, that I may not thirst, nor come here to draw," begged the woman.

"Go, call your husband, and come here."

"I have no husband."

"You are right in saying, 'I have no husband,'" Jesus said to her, "for you have had five husbands, and he whom you now have is not your husband; this you said truly."

"Sir, I perceive that you are a prophet. Our fathers worshiped on this mountain; and you say that in Jerusalem is the place where men ought to worship."

"Woman, believe me, the hour is coming, and now is, when the true worshipers will worship the Father in spirit and truth."

The woman said to him, "I know that Messiah is coming; when he comes, he will show us all things."

And Jesus answered, "I who speak to you am he."

The Samaritan woman, who had chosen to take water out of the well alone in the afternoon, so she would not be insulted by her neighbours who called her an adulteress, had just had the first revelation from the son of Mary. Nobody until then had heard anything like it. She had just witnessed a show of belief in himself by this Man who by now had no doubt as to his true nature.

The last disciples

Many of the Samaritans were converted when they found out what had happened in the well. But Jesus had to keep walking. A month later he was on the shores of the Sea of Galilee, perhaps to get back four of his disciples who had gone back to their work as fishermen instead of following him.

It was not hard to find Peter, who was mending fishing nets. He asked him for a boat to use as a sort of pulpit, and spoke from it to the crowd. At the end of his preaching he said to Peter:

"The time has come for your work as fishermen to be done. Put out into the deep and let down your nets for a catch."

"Master, we toiled all night and took nothing. But at your word I will let down the nets."

But Jesus' gaze was so crystal clear that Peter regretted his doubts. He ordered his companions to follow him in another boat. They threw their nets out into the water and straight away realised that they were full to breaking point.

The boats were so heavy with fish they were nearly sinking, but their crew managed to take them to the shore. As soon as they got there, Peter kneeled before Jesus and said in sorrow:

"Depart from me, for I am a sinful man, O Lord."

"Do not be afraid; henceforth you will be catching men."

He made Andrew, James and John a similar offer. He then had the unconditional support of these four disciples. All of them left their usual occupations to follow him selflessly.

The Sermon on the Mount

Jesus went up on a mountain to speak in his usual way. He often chose the most isolated places in the towns or villages he came to. He spent the night on the mount, and in the morning settled himself on the gentle slope. Several hundred men and women surrounded him, and he said to them:

Blessed are the poor in spirit, for theirs is the kingdom of heaven.

Blessed are the meek, for they shall inherit the earth.

Blessed are those who mourn, for they shall be comforted.

Blessed are those who hunger and thirst for righteousness, for they will be satisfied.

Blessed are the merciful, for they will obtain mercy.

Blessed are the pure in heart, for they shall see God.

Blessed are the peacemakers, for they will be called the children of God.

Blessed are those who are persecuted for righteousness' sake, for theirs is the kingdom of heaven.

Blessed are you when men revile you and persecute you and utter all kinds of evil against you falsely on my account. Rejoice and be glad, for your reward is great in heaven.

Jesus preaching on the Mount

All of them understood these blessings. But the Master followed with a more enigmatic message.

"You are the salt of the earth; but if salt has lost its taste, how shall its saltness be restored? He continued the sermon and came to another enigmatic passage: "You are the light of the world..."

He went on to give many of the rules of his doctrine: respect for the spirit of justice to enter into heaven, not insulting your brother, rejecting adultery with thought itself ("If your right eye causes you to sin, pluck it out... and if your right hand causes you to sin, cut it off..."), loving your neighbour, and praying for your enemies, among other things.

And so he gave form to the most human doctrine the world has ever known. In essence, it perfected other previous religions: Akhenaton, Buddha, Confucius, the Essenians, etc., for they had sown the seeds. The 'salt of the earth' is a symbol of what gives food its flavour, and at the same time represents such a strong link that not even God can break it. The same meaning should be given to the phrase, "You are the light of the world."

CHAPTER VII

MIRACLES AND WORDS

The centurion's servant

Jesus was still being followed by the crowds when he came to Capernaum. There was a strategically placed Roman barracks there, at the crossing of the paths leading from the Euphrates and Syria to the port of Caesarea and also to Jerusalem and Egypt.

It was there that he met a Roman centurion, who had become well known for loving the Jews when he paid for the construction of a synagogue. He knew of Christ's miracles and went to him to ask him to heal one of his servants who was lying ill in bed:

"Lord, my servant is lying paralysed at home, in terrible distress," he said humbly.

"I will come and heal him," said Jesus.

Suddenly, a declaration of absolute faith was heard:

"Lord, I am not worthy to have you come under my roof; but only say the word, and my servant will be healed. For I am a man under authority, with soldiers under me; and I say to one, 'Go,' and he goes, and to another, 'Come,' and he comes, and to my slave, 'Do this,' and he does it.

The Master looked at him in admiration.

"Truly I say to you, not even in Israel have I found such faith. I tell you, many will come from east and west and sit at table with Abraham, Isaac, and Jacob in the kingdom of heaven, while the sons of the kingdom will be thrown into the outer darkness…"

Next, he said to the centurion, "Go; be it done for you as you have believed."

Just then, the servant was healed and rose from his sickbed. This was one of the most moving moments in Jesus' life, and proved that foreigners or those who were not children of Israel were often more receptive to his message, less mediated by an absolutist religion.

The transfiguration of Jesus

In the Gospel according to Saint Matthew (17;1-13) the following is written:

And after six days Jesus took with him Peter and James and John his brother, and led them up a high mountain apart. And he was transfigured before them, and his face shone like the sun, and his garments became white as light. And behold, there appeared to them Moses and Elijah, talking with him. And Peter said to Jesus, "Lord, it is well that we are here; if you wish, I will make three booths here, one for you and one for Moses and one for Elijah." He was still speaking, when lo, a bright cloud overshadowed them, and a voice from the cloud said, "This is my beloved Son, which whom I am well pleased; listen to him." When the disciples heard this, they fell on their faces, and were filled with awe. But Jesus came and touched them, saying, "Rise, and have no fear." And when they lifted up their eyes, they saw no one but Jesus only.

And as they were coming down the mountain, Jesus commanded them, "Tell no one the vision, until the Son of man is raised from the dead." And the disciples asked him, "Then why do the scribes say that first Elijah must come?" He replied, "Elijah does come, and he is to restore all things;

but I tell you that Elijah has already come, and they did not know him, but did to him whatever they pleased. So also the Son of man will suffer at their hands." Then the disciples understood that he was speaking to them of John the Baptist.

A quick look at the transfiguration

The transfiguration on Mount Tabor was a manifestation of Jesus' divinity. For a few moments he was God, and that is why the two great patriarchs of Israel had come to speak to him. It was the best way for the three privileged disciples to be sure that they were following the bearer of the Truth.

All the rest are symbols that make the event extremely important: the cloud should be seen as an announcement of the presence of Yahweh, as he used it to communicate with Moses and other great men; the shining of Jesus' clothing makes him like the angels or the heavens, and God himself speaks: this is the ultimate revelation of Jesus Christ's divinity, perhaps more important than his baptism in the river Jordan.

Many biographies on Christ ignore this passage, because it shows he was God. As what they want to show is that he was a Man, the greatest man of all, they try to avoid conferring on him a divine nature. Our idea here is to show that the transfiguration makes the image of the Human Being that Jesus was even greater.

After the events on Mount Tabor, the Son of Man behaved as he always had. He was still himself. If he realised what lie before him, he did not often show it.

A demand for miracles

While they were in Capernaum, Simon the disciple was told that his mother was in bed with a high fever. Jesus was taken to the house to work miracles.

This, however, was a role he was not prepared to take on – that of a magician or miracle worker. His way of converting was through the word, the most effective way to get his message clearly across.

Yet before the exacting gaze of those present, he saw that he had to comply with them. He felt the desire to do so more strongly when he saw that the old woman was sending him a sincere message of faith. He took her hands between his and ordered her:

"Woman, get up out of your bed, and finish the tasks you left undone."

She got up immediately with renewed agility and went straight into the kitchen. In her smile could be seen her thanks to her healer.

This miracle was added to the fishing miracle, and the healing of the possessed man, and this made demand for Jesus' work grow. A few hours later Simon was surrounded by the injured, the crippled and the blind as well as those with incurable illnesses wanting to be healed.

Jesus told them gently that he would not be able to help them, hoping they would not leave full of despair if he softened his words. Over the next few days he healed only those who he thought would be able to keep the miracle secret, and did not appear in public again until he was far away from Capernaum.

A torrent of love

Jesus was surrounded by humble people wherever he went, and let his love flow over them. Peace was his message. He did not hate anybody or seek verbal or physical confrontation. His teachings came from his heart.

"[God] makes his sun rise on the evil and on the good, and sends rain on the just and the unjust. Those who believe in Him will possess the kingdom of heaven on earth. Ask, and it will be given you; seek, and you will find; knock, and it will be opened to you."

Jesus healing the sick (drawing by Rembrandt)

'These were such different words to the priests', especially when they proclaimed vengeance, "an eye for an eye and a tooth for a tooth." The preacher of love advised them:

"If anyone strikes you on the right cheek, turn to him the other also; and if anyone would sue you and take our coat, let him have your cloak as well."

When his listeners started thinking that this was too much, Jesus added, to calm them,

"For if you forgive men their trespasses, your heavenly Father also will forgive you."

Then he complicated things by adding something questionable: "Love your enemies, do good to those who hate you, bless those who curse you, pray for those who abuse you."

This idea was so difficult to grasp that one of the listeners asked, "Lord, how often shall my brother sin against me, and I forgive him? As many as seven times"

"I do not say to you seven times, but seventy times seven."

Confusion took over and it seemed they were being spoken to by a madman or a believer in lost causes. But Jesus knew what they were thinking, and soon brought them round to him again:

"Judge not and you will not be judged. So whatever you wish that men would do to you, do so to them; for this is the law and the prophets."

A sigh of relief came with the peoples' approval. They nodded, as they had understood this message of fraternal love. They were all in search of a superior destiny. Was it not absurd to let negative feelings predominate when eternal life in love was waiting for them?

Preaching by Example

Jesus accepted invitations from the poorest people, but before sitting down at the table, he always took care of the animals in the stable, and greeted the children and old people. He also carried firewood or water and did other domestic tasks. He did all this so naturally that his guests were predisposed to believe him when he said:

Blessed are you, the poor, for yours is the kingdom of God. Do not lay up for yourselves treasures on earth, where moth and rust consume and where thieves break in and steal, but lay up for yourselves treasures in heaven. For where your treasure is, there will your heart be also.

Galilee was an area where no one had very much financial security, as there were too many friends of other's belongings. His example was exact and easy to understand, and they trusted him.

"When you give a dinner or a banquet, do not invite your friends or your brothers or your kinsmen or rich neighbours, lest they also invite you in return, and you be repaid. But when you give a feast, invite the poor, the maimed, the lame, the blind, and you will be blessed, because they cannot repay you. You will be repaid at the resurrection of the just."

Most of those listening were gratified by this message, but not those who were rich or who enjoyed throwing feasts to show off their wealth. One of these, a young man, said:

"Teacher, all these I have observed from my youth."

"You lack one thing; go, sell what you have, and give to the poor."

The young man found the words offensive and looked at Jesus with disdain. He left the place with his head held high. He might have just heard the words his reaction deserved:

"Children, how hard it is to enter the kingdom of God! It is easier for a camel to go through the eye of a needle than for a rich man to enter the kingdom of God."

Two delightful parables

Jesus favoured sinners and this often surprised those who saw him. His disciples did not dare to openly reproach him for this, but they deserved a lesson. Jesus told them two delightful parables that they understood perfectly:

"Which man of you, having a hundred sheep, if he has lost one of them, does not leave the ninety-nine in the wilderness, and go after the one which is lost, until he finds it? And when he has found it, he lays it on his shoulders, rejoicing. And when he comes home, he calls together his friends and his neighbours, saying to them, 'Rejoice with me, for I have found my sheep which was lost.' Just so, I tell you, there will be more joy in heaven over one sinner who repents than over ninety-nine righteous persons who need no repentance."

Next, he told them the parable of the Prodigal Son, who asked his father for his part of the inheritance and went off to squander it in far-away lands. When he found himself left with nothing, he went back home, where his father was waiting for him with open arms. As soon as he was by his side, he kissed him, had him bathed and anointed, and then dressed him in his best clothing and ordered the fatted calf to be killed. Then, the other son, who had worked hard in his father's house all along, felt so unfairly treated that he protested. The father replied, "Son, you are always with me, and all that is mine is yours. It was fitting to make merry and be glad, for this your brother was dead, and is alive; he was lost, and is found.?

These two parables were well understood by those who were parents and anybody who tended animals. Other people needed to discuss them, finding it hard to accept that goodness deserved no reward. Soon they understood that the message was more subtle than that, because there is no greater pain than seeing a loved one lost forever.

Parables had been used since ancient times. Many civilisations had used them, particularly the Egyptians and the Buddhists. But they did not usually have such a direct interpretation, except for the 'elephant and the blind men' attributed to Buddha. A group of blind men were asked to touch different parts of an elephant and afterwards to say what they thought the animal was like. Those who touched its leg said it was a strong column; those who had felt its body thought it was like a great stone, and so on. The moral of this story is that the truth can only be perceived when something is examined in all its facets.

One of the moments in the parable of the Prodigal Son

The first attack against the holy men

As was mentioned previously, Jesus was causing a revolution, going against established norms in Israeli society. However peaceful his acts were, when he spoke, he always led people to strongly criticise different social strata. His criticism of the rich had turned many of them against him. The worst thing was when he had started to criticise the religious behaviour of the Jews, going against the holy men.

"Beware of practising your piety before men in order to be seen by them; for then you will have no reward from your Father who is in heaven.

"Thus, when you give alms, sound no trumpet before you, as the hypocrites do in the synagogues and in the streets, that they may be praised by men. Truly, I say to you, they have received their reward. But when you give alms, do not let your left hand know what your right hand is doing, so that your alms may be in secret; and your Father who sees in secret will reward you.

"And when you pray, you must not be like the hypocrites; for they love to stand and pray in the synagogues and at the street corners, that they may be seen by men. But when you pray, go into your room and shut the door and pray to your Father who is in secret.

"And when you fast, do not look dismal, like the hypocrites, for they disfigure their faces that their fasting may be seen by men. But when you fast, anoint your head and wash your face, that your fasting may not be seen by men.

"If you are offering your gift at the altar, and there remember that your brother has something against you, leave your gift there before the altar and go; first be reconciled to your brother, and then come and offer your gift."

The phrase 'something against you' was full of references, especially for those who thought they had no need to repent when they went into the temples feeling no guilt: for example, having disobeyed the commandment "You shall not covet your neighbour's wife."

It was not just the adulterous in thought who felt wounded by this allusion. The holy men went to complain to the Sanhedrin as well. For the time being, the judges did no more than listen without taking any action. Nicodemus decided not to intervene on Jesus' behalf, but did send a message to the disciples, entreating them to be more careful.

Sin is a disease of the spirit

Whenever Jesus healed a sick person, he ended the session by saying "Go, and sin no more." Some people did not understand this as they did not realise that physical and spiritual health went together. It was enough just to look at the Master to see this: he was always agile, alert and in high spirits, as he was the fairest and most well balanced man ever seen. He was one who could say things like this:

"Do not be anxious about your life, what you shall eat or what you shall drink, nor about your body, what you shall put on. Is not life more than food, and the body more than clothing? Look at the birds of the air: they neither sow nor reap nor gather into barns, and yet your heavenly Father feeds them. Are you not of more value than they? Consider the lilies of the field, how they grow; they neither toil nor spin; yet I tell you, even Solomon in all his glory was not arrayed like one of these. But if God so clothes the grass of the field, which today is alive and tomorrow is thrown into the oven, will he not much more clothe you, O men of little faith? Therefore do not be anxious about tomorrow, for tomorrow will be anxious for itself. Let the day's own trouble be sufficient for the day."

Each of these words was filled with sincerity. Jesus did not plan his days. When he awoke at sunrise, after washing and dressing, he left his disciples to decide on the path to follow. He was always satisfied with what he had to eat, whether it was a lot or little. This surprised some people, and they said to him,

"Why [did John the Baptist's followers] and the Pharisees fast, but your disciples do not fast?"

"Can the wedding guests mourn as long as the bridegroom is with them? The days will come, when the bridegroom is taken away from them, and then they will fast."

Jesus' life then was one of joy and cheer and none of his followers had to go through any kind of deprivation. Nobody washed their plates more than once, and nobody was too preoccupied with the cleanliness the Jewish rituals dictated. The disciples knew the Lord's Prayer but only said it occasionally when they thought it was a good idea.

Love of children

The Son of Man, as he called himself then, preached that the Good Times would come into peoples' hearts naturally, with no other pressure than truth and cleanness of spirit.

Who were more prepared to see this than children? He loved their innocence, just as he sought the ignorant to teach them and the humble who had not been corrupted by riches. One day when his disciples were turning away mothers who tried to bring their children to him, Jesus exclaimed:

"Let the children come to me, do not hinder them; for to such belongs the kingdom of God. Truly I say to you, whoever does not receive the kingdom of God like a child shall not enter it."

When they were near him he would watch them play, feeling the world around them as children do. Did there exist a flower in the world more beautiful than a child acting naturally and innocently?

A small commune

Jesus and his disciples' life together can be seen as a small commune, where the only things needed were fidelity, respect for the Lord's word and not having any money of one's own. All coins were placed in a communal pot, something the Essenians had been doing for centuries. The administrator is thought to have been Judas, the most practical one of the group.

One morning, when they were walking along the beach, Jesus saw a customs official in his office. Then, he realised that the parable of the Prodigal Son could be applied in real life. He went up to the man, Matthew Levi, an ex-disciple who had decided to go back to his job as a tax collector, and asked him to follow him. He obeyed immediately and this made Jesus glad.

Most of Jesus' followers were Galileans. Now we know that some women accompanied him but very seldom joined the men. Some historians do say that in the first years, Peter and other disciples took their wives with them, but this is not easy to ascertain.

Jesus also rejected many of those who asked to be disciples, following an intuition that they would not be loyal to him. How then did he allow Judas to come to be by his side? Was he obeying a foreordained script or a prophecy? Did he know beforehand that someone would betray him and bring him to his tragic end?

Many other questions might well be asked at this point but we will leave this matter here.

To relieve the tension, we will say that Jesus gave his disciples many names, such as sons, workers, fishers of men, etc.

A closer look at the disciples

The disciples were neither poor nor uneducated. Their professions would appear to place them in the middle class. The fishermen among them had their own boats with space for crews of thirteen. This meant they had employees whom they had to sell their boats to before following the Lord.

Matthew-Levi was a civil servant in the Tax Office and should be considered a tax collector. Judas was also an educated man, enough so to be in charge of the group's accounts. John was the only single man among them. Peter had a wife and children. We must remember that this extremely important disciple was called Simon until Jesus changed his name. He dedicated to him the famous phrase:

"I tell you, you are Peter, and on this rock I will build my church, and the powers of death shall not prevail against it."

It is thought that there were twelve disciples following Jesus, though they were rarely all together by their master's side. It has been said that there were in fact seventy-two or more of them. Each of them gave money to the 'community', although the main earnings came from the donations of women who followed this privileged group of men.

Were the Pharisees his worst enemies?

Some historians defend the Pharisees for being the most orthodox Jews, those who stuck most obstinately to their religious principles. When Jesus came along they put up defensive barriers that the Christians considered criminal. There were certainly bad Pharisees, such as those who were called 'whitewashed tombs'.

Actually, most of them did not like Jesus, and he treated them as the enemies they were. Right from the beginning he was aware that they were spying on him. Yet this did not stop him from speaking to them and even accepting invitations to share their tables.

One day he was celebrating a feast to which certain tax collectors and sinners had been invited, and the Pharisees asked one of the disciples:

"Why does your teacher eat with tax collectors and sinners?"

On hearing these words, Jesus shouted violently,

Jesus at one of the pagan feasts

"Those who are well have no need of a physician, but those who are sick. Go and learn what this means. For I came not to call the righteous, but sinners."

This was such an effective attack that the Pharisees left, unable to come up with an appropriate retort. But they were never to forget this initial public humiliation. How could they get retribution?

Their complaints to the Sanhedrin had no effect because Jesus had done nothing that could be considered sinful against the official religion. Anyone could speak in public, even if some of the contents of the sacred books were criticised. However, they thought Jesus should be surrounded by spies in the hope that he might make a critical mistake.

They still did not think he was as dangerous as John the Baptist, who was still shut away in the dungeons of Herod Antipas. If he became more seditious, they trusted that he would be treated in a similar way.

CHAPTER VIII

THE END OF THE JOYFUL TIMES

The accumulation of 'sins'

Jesus continued to follow his day-to-day needs. One morning, when he was walking through wheat fields with his disciples, some of them felt hungry and broke off some shoots to eat. The Pharisees who were following them said:

"Look, why are they doing what is not lawful on the Sabbath."

Saturday was still the Jews' holy day, and absolute rest was obligatory, except for going to the temple or holding the compulsory rituals. Any kind of work was forbidden, and Jesus and his followers' behaviour seemed like work.

"Have you not read what David did , when he was in need and was hungry, he and those who were with him: how he entered the house of God, and ate the bread of the Presence, which is not lawful for any but the priests to eat? The Sabbath was made for man, not man for the Sabbath; so the Son of man is lord even of the Sabbath."

The Pharisees went off feeling satisfied, for they had witnessed a sin or a profanation.

Hours later, some men came up to Jesus with a paralysed man. It was impossible for them to get to him as he was surrounded by a crowd that completely blocked their way. They improvised a stretcher and lifted him over their heads, shouting for people to let them through. As soon as the Lord saw the paralysed man, he surprised them all by saying, "My son, your sins are forgiven!"

"This man is blaspheming! Only God can forgive sin!"

"Why do you think evil in your hearts?" Jesus asked his enemies after knowing their thoughts. "For which is easier to say, 'Your sins are forgiven,' or to say, 'Rise and walk'?" As soon as he said this, the paralysed man got to his feet, put his stretcher over his shoulders and walked through the human passage that was opening up. They were all so astonished that not one of them dared to express his jubilation. They were actually in another state altogether: amazement at the unexplainable.

Could what they had just seen be explained as an act of magic or a true miracle? Did they really have the Messiah before them, or was he a prophet, or a superior being to everything reflected in the Scriptures?

Meanwhile, the Pharisees were again so smug and satisfied at having witnessed another sin or blasphemy. Anyone who considered himself equal to God deserved death. The Sanhedrin could by now take action against Jesus, but did not dare – the judge Nicodemus had managed to convince his colleagues that the people of Palestine's love for Jesus would cause an uprising if they did so.

In actual fact, once the first impression any miracle caused had passed, reason came in and worked to the benefit of the Son of Man who healed the incurable without demanding anything in return.

Playing with fire

Jesus never felt afraid of the Pharisees... or was he not perhaps intentionally playing with fire with his provocation? The parable he told a few days later was very dangerous:

Jesus curing a sick man (drawing by Rembrandt)

"Two men went up into the temple to pray, one a Pharisee and the other a tax collector. The Pharisee stood and prayed thus with himself, 'God, I thank thee that I am not like other men, extortioners, unjust, adulterers, or even like this tax collector. I fast twice a week, I give tithes of all that I get.' But the tax collector, standing far off, would not even lift up his eyes to heaven, but beat his breast, saying, 'God, be merciful to me a sinner!' I tell you, this man went down to his house justified rather than the other; for every one who exalts himself will be humbled, but he who humbles himself will be exalted."

This parable made Jesus known in Galilee as an enemy of the Pharisees. The poor were comforted by it, assured by a defender, while those he had alluded to continued to take note of his 'sins', trusting that one day there would be so many of them that the Sanhedrin would have to act to quieten the rebel.

The parable of the Good Samaritan

The Son of Man was in Judea when he was challenged by a doctor of the Law.

"Teacher, what shall I do to inherit eternal life?"

"What is written in the law?"

"You shall love the Lord your God with all your heart, and with all your soul, and with all your strength, and with all you mind; and your neighbour as yourself."

"You have answered right; do this, and you will live."

"And who is my neighbour?" insisted the lawyer trying to catch Jesus out.

"A man was going down from Jerusalem to Jericho, and he fell among robbers, who stripped him and beat him, and departed, leaving him half dead. Now by chance a priest was going down that road; and when he saw him he passed by on the other side. So likewise a Levite, when he came to the place and saw him, passed by on the other side. But a Samaritan, as he journeyed, came to where he was; and when he saw him, he had compassion, and went to him and bound up his wounds, pouring on oil and wine; then he set him on his own beast and brought him to an inn, and took care of him. And the next day he took out two denarii and gave them to the innkeeper, saying, 'Take care of him; and whatever more you spend, I will repay you when I come back.' Which of these three, do you think, proved neighbour to the man who fell among the robbers?" The man said, "The one who showed mercy on him." And Jesus said to him, "Go and do likewise."

This parable told by the Son of Man, a revolutionary, can be considered the straw that broke the camel's back. He had chosen a Samaritan, a race considered in Palestine to be 'beneath contempt', as the best of the three men, and had insulted two representatives of the upper bourgeoisie.

A death threat for Jesus

The Pharisees, scribes and some rich Jews were prepared to prove that Jesus was a trick artist, and had become involved in a argument with him that they took care to suffuse with verbal violence, while he only answered with the truth. Their aggressiveness reached the point of insult when one of his enemies asked him:

"Are we not right in saying that you are a Samaritan and have a demon?"

Jesus answered, "I have not a demon; but I honour my Father, and you dishonour me. Yet I do not seek my own glory; there is One who seeks it and he will be the judge. Truly, truly, I say to you, if any one keeps my word, he will never see death."

"Now we know that you have a demon. Abraham died, as did the prophets; and you say, 'If any one keeps my word, he will never taste death.' Are you greater than our father Abraham, who died? And the prophets died! Who de you claim to be?"

"If I glorify myself, my glory is nothing; it is my Father who glorifies me, of whom you say that he is your God. But you have not known him; I know him. If I said, I do not know him, I should be a liar like you; but I do know him and I keep his word. Your father Abraham rejoiced that he was to see my day; he saw it and was glad."

Then the Jews thought they had heard enough. Their speaker shouted:

"You are not yet fifty years old, and have you seen Abraham?"

"Truly, truly, I say to you, before Abraham was, I am."

Then Jesus' enemies armed themselves with stones to throw at him. They were prepared to kill him for blasphemy. But they did not even raise their arms, because he disappeared. The day of his sacrifice had not yet come.

Mary Magdalene

Months later, another Pharisee invited Jesus and he accepted. While they were eating, a very beautiful woman appeared. Her name was Mary Magdalene, and she was a prostitute who had slept with almost all the men there. They tried to get rid of her by mocking her, but she was determined to meet the merciful man from Nazareth. As soon as she saw his sweet gaze, so different from the mocking looks that followed her, she knelt before him. With tears of happiness she bathed his feet, taken by an impulse she was afraid might offend him. So she looked for a cloth to dry him with.

When she could not find one, she used her long hair and her lips. Then she anointed his feet with ointment she took from an alabaster container she always carried. But shame would not allow her to raise her head, thinking she was not worthy of such a great Man. Suddenly, the Pharisee decided this was a chance to shame his enemy.

"If you were truly a prophet, you would know that this woman is a sinner."

Jesus refrained from answering his attacker. Instead, he spoke to Peter of the parable of the two men who both owed money to a creditor. The creditor pardoned them their debts, but they were not of the same amount, as one had a very large debt while the other's was relatively small. To end, he asked who was most thankful.

"The one, I suppose, to whom he forgave more," answered the disciple.

"You have judged rightly." He paused. He looked at the woman and then at the Pharisee and said, "Do you see this woman? I entered your house, you gave me no water for my feet, but she has wet my feet with her tears and wiped them with her hair. You gave me no kiss, but from the time I cam in she has not ceased to kiss my feet. You did not anoint my head with oil, but she has anointed my feet with ointment. Therefore I tell you, her sins, which are many, are forgiven, for she loved much; but he who is forgiven little, loves little."

The guests at the party remained silent, unable to react. Meanwhile, Mary Magdalene and Jesus continued to do as they had been: she, the sinner, anointed his feet and he, who had never known a woman, accepted her treatment which dignified them both.

Shortly afterwards, Jesus got up and the repented woman did the same. He said to her:

"Your sins are forgiven. Your faith has saved you; go in peace."

And she did so, but only then. After that she was to become one of the women that followed Jesus. And as she had been healed by a divine doctor, she would never again have sexual relations with any man, and nor would she feel any shame when many of those she rejected reminded her of her past. It is possible she understood his message even better than any of the disciples; for this very reason she did not abandon him, even on the cross.

Legion, the possessed Hercules

Months later, Jesus and his disciples met near the mouth of the River Jordan. These were lands where herds of pigs roamed, and it was unpleasant to see. They were surprised, however, when they came upon a repulsive man. Dirty hair covered his head, he was dressed in shabby skins covering only a third of his body, and he looked like an inhuman Hercules. He had apparently been chained many times in a cave, but had always managed to break his bonds, whether they were thick cords or chains. Lately he roamed free, and chased away anyone who came near him by hurling stones at them.

After what we have told, therefore, it is not surprising that he was received by fear from the crowds when he arrived at the master's side. But he seemed quite aware when he asked:

"What have you to do with me, Jesus, Son of the Most High God? I adjure you by God, do not torment me."

"What is your name?" asked Christ.

"My name is Legion."

The Master placed his hands on the kneeling man's shoulders and lightly shook his whole body. The two of them stared at each other, and Jesus' will was stronger than the possessed man's. This was the best way to cure him of his possession. However...

The crowd's attention had been captured by the shouts of a swineherd and then by the noise of the pigs falling into water. It was a simple accident, set off by the swine herd's distraction. He had been watching what was occurring in the valley and had forgotten that the pigs were very close to a cliff, with a lake at the bottom.

Superstitious people thought that the demons that had been expelled from Legion's body had gone into the pigs. This filled them with terror, and after getting together to speak of the matter, they went to beg Jesus and his disciples to leave. They were forbidden from going into the city.

The Good Samaritan (drawing by Rembrandt)

The Pharisees continue their persecution

The Pharisees were already waiting for Jesus when he arrived in Galilee. Two days later, when they saw him walking down a crowded street, they asked him:

"Master, when will the kingdom of heaven come?"

They spoke so maliciously that the disciples thought there would be no answer. They were completely mistaken. The Son of Man used the occasion to teach the crowds a lesson and also show the Pharisees that he was not afraid of them.

"The kingdom of God will never arrive unexpectedly or cause your eyes to marvel. You will hear no one. It is already here. I tell you that the kingdom of God is among you."

He went on his way and left the Pharisees in a state of indignation. They had nothing to reproach him this time, as his words contained nothing that sinned against the official religion of Israel.

The following day, some other Pharisees tried to provoke Jesus with a poisonous question:

"Why do you not show us a sign from heaven, master?"

The Son of Man did not react with his usual calmness this time. He looked at his aggressors and answered sourly:

"When it is evening, you say, 'It will be fair weather; for the sky is red.' And in the morning, 'It will be stormy today, for the sky is red and threatening.' You know how to interpret the appearance of the sky, but you cannot interpret the signs of the times. An evil and adulterous generation seeks for a sign, but no sign shall be given to it."

These words sounded so aggressive that people were alarmed and urged the Pharisees to leave . They left, but were satisfied as they had managed to anger the man they continuously persecuted in search of new sins or crimes to present to the Sanhedrin.

The sleeping 'dead woman'

Jesus once again found himself at Capernaum, where he had been solicited by Jairus, a weeping rabbi whose body was hunched up in pain like an old man's. His voice, however, was full of faith.

"My little daughter is at the point of death. Come and lay your hands on her, so that she may be made well and live."

This conviction in the mouth of a man from the enemy castes was rewarded. They soon reached the man's home, from which emerged shouts anguish: "Your daughter is dead!"

The miracle of Jarius' daughter (drawing by Rembrandt)

Jesus took no notice of the voices, sure that this was just a superstitious reaction that could take catalepsy for death. He approached the bed, where the young girl was lying as if dead, and asked the women sobbing around her:

"Why do you make a tumult and weep? The child is not dead but sleeping."

Some made sarcastic comments, and the Master asked for everyone to leave. Once he was alone with the father, the two of them standing next to the bed, he said to him:

"Do not fear; only believe and she shall be well." And he took the girl by the hand and said, "Child, arise," and her spirit returned, and she got up at once.

And so the young girl overcame death as if it were just a dream. Neither the rabbi Jairus nor the humble people were ever to forget this true miracle.

The death of John the Baptist

John the Baptist had been held in Herod's dungeons for a long time. At times he was allowed fairly frequent visits, and his followers were led to believe he might be set free. His relationship with Jesus through common friends was probably quite constant. We know they were distant cousins, but they were united more by firm beliefs that neither of them was prepared to deny.

For this very reason John was beheaded, although the story holds it as a whim of Herodias, the tyrant's wife, and Salome. The crime caused commotion throughout all of Palestine. Jesus was also deeply affected, and not only lamented the death of his 'brother', but also hardened his sermons and increased his attacks on the corrupt political and religious classes of Israel.

He had never attacked them directly and he still did not do this, but instead continued to use words and a few concrete

112

measures, such as not respecting the Sabbath, or not observing table rituals and other impositions he considered absurd. His first contact with people was filled with demonstrations of love and brotherhood and took place in a joyful atmosphere, although towards the end he became more austere.

CHAPTER IX

I AM THE MESSIAH!

The calling of Martha and Mary

In Bethany there was a family of two sisters and one brother who were friends of Jesus: Mary, Martha and Lazarus. The two women had followed Jesus among the others but had had to return home when they found out that Lazarus was very ill. They first tried to cure him with traditional remedies, but when they realised their efforts were futile, they sent someone they knew to ask Jesus for help. As always, he calmed them with his words:

"This illness is not unto death; it is for the glory of God, so that the Son of God may be glorified by means of it."

It was clear now that there was no time to waste. He waited for two days, and when the third day came, he said to his disciples:

"Let us go into Judea again."

"Rabbi, the Jews were but now seeking to stone you, and are you going there again?" Peter asked, afraid.

Jesus answered, "Are there not twelve hours in the day? If any one walks in the day, he does not stumble, because he sees the light of this world. But if any one walks in the night, he stumbles, because the light is not in him." These words calmed the disciples, and he added, "Our friend Lazarus has fallen asleep, but I go to awake him out of sleep."

"Lord, if he has fallen asleep, he will recover," said Thomas, thinking that the Master meant taking rest in sleep.

"Lazarus is dead; let us go to him," said Jesus.

"Let us also go, that we may die with him," said Thomas.

Lazarus in his tomb

Before Jesus got to Bethany, about two miles from Jerusalem, Martha came out to tell him that her brother had already been buried for four days. Full of faith, she continued:

"Lord, if you had been here, my brother would not have died. And even now I know that whatever you ask from God, God will give you."

Jesus said to her, "Your brother will rise again."

Martha responded, "I know that he will rise again in the resurrection at the last day."

"I am the resurrection and the life; he who believes in me, though he die, yet shall he live, and whoever lives and believes in me shall never die. Do you believe this?"

"Yes, Lord; I believe that you are the Christ, the Son of God, he who is coming into the world."

Martha felt so comforted that, begging their pardon for leaving, went off to look for her sister Mary. She ran quickly home and when she went through the door tried to disguise her panting, as she wished to keep her news a secret. But there were too many people there, and some of them realised that Mary had gone out. They followed her, thinking that she was going to the tomb of her beloved brother.

By the time the two women got to where Jesus was, just outside the city, they had about a dozen Jews with them.

"Lord, if you had been here, my brother would not have died," said Mary, unable to contain her tears.

The two sisters and their followers were weeping so sorrowfully that the Son of Man asked:

"Where have you laid him?"

"Lord, come and see," answered Martha.

Then Jesus' eyes filled with tears. He had truly loved Lazarus, but some people took this as a sign of weakness and whispered:

"Could not he who opened the eyes of the blind man have kept this man from dying?"

The greatest miracle of all

Jesus was deeply moved. He may have been weeping for the four days that Lazarus had been buried. When he came before the tomb, he ordered:

"Take away the stone."

"Lord, by this time there will be an odour, for he has been dead four days," said Martha.

"Did I not tell you that if you would believe you would see the glory of God?" asked Jesus in a voice that only allowed one decision to be made.

They moved the enormous stone that had been rolled over as a door. Then, Jesus turned his gaze to the heavens and said:

"Father, I thank thee that thou hast heard me. I knew that thou hearest me always, but I have said this on account of the people standing by, that they may believe that thou didst send me." Next, he looked inside the sepulchre and called:

"Lazarus, come out!"

At that very instant the supposedly dead man came out of the sepulchre-cave, with his legs and hands tied with bandages and his face covered in a shroud. Jesus advised the two sisters:

"Unbind him, and let him go."

Soon Lazarus appeared before them all as vigorous as a young man. He thanked his saviour for giving him back his life and then returned home arm in arm with his two sisters, who were weeping for joy.

All those present were amazed and firmly believed in Jesus. However, the enemies of the Nazarene who had disguised themselves among the crowd ran to inform the Sanhedrin, as this miracle was considered an act of magic.

There is not doubt we have just described the greatest of the miracles Jesus ever performed. Such a colossal event as this would have served to finally sanctify he who had worked it, although in a different country. Lazarus was a rich man, perhaps a Pharisee (he was one of the few, apart from Nicodemus, who defended Jesus), and his resurrection should have been seen as proof of the Truth. However...

Israel was blind

José Luis Martín Descalzo, in his book *Vida y misterio de Jesús de Nazaret* (*The Life and Mystery of Jesus of Nazareth*) tells us clearly that:

They did not have eyes in their heads. The final proof was before them, they had seen a man who had been dead for four days arise with the uttering of three simple words; it had happened during the day, in front of numerous witnesses, both friendly and hostile; the resuscitated man was before them, and they could speak to him and touch his hands. But their only conclusion was that they would have to kill the miracle worker and eliminate the evidence.

It is this blindness that makes Jesus weep. One day, the city sleeping beneath his feet would be devastated because it did not want or know how to understand. And the most important people in the city will be held responsible; those very people who went to Bethany, sure that Jesus would not dare to act in their sight and left with their hearts hardened and the decision made.

Jesus with Martha and Mary (drawing by Rembrandt)

And Jesus sees the city destroyed, burned to the ground, with no stone left standing. And he weeps, for he loves this city as he loved Lazarus. But he knows that if he can win over death and the corruption of the flesh, he is helpless in the face of a spirit that does not want to see. He is the resurrection and the life, but only for those who believe in him. Lazarus was really asleep. His soul was not defiled and did not stink of corruption. The Pharisees, who would later return to their homes, thought they were alive. But their souls stank worse than Lazarus' tomb.

The Son of Man was ahead of his time when he envisioned the destruction of Jerusalem that would take place many years later. We now know that the religion of Israel did not accept Jesus, in spite of all his prodigies and his humanitarian message, the most democratic one the world had ever known until then. His tears should also be taken to show his enormous frustration, for he had offered his doctrine to the chosen people of God, and was heard only by the humble. Also, the greater his prodigies, the closer his execution came – the greatest injustice ever to be committed in the history of the world.

The healing of the blind man

This particular miracle came long before the resurrection of Lazarus, but we have decided to speak about it here in order to show how obsessively stubborn the enemies of Truth were. They would not believe in it however close it came, however visible it was and however much it directly affected them.

One afternoon when Jesus and his disciples were walking by the temple, they saw a man begging who had been blind from birth. Peter asked him:

"Rabbi, who sinned, this man or his parents, that he was born blind?"

He was questioning the eternal mystery of human birth and how people could be born with serious disabilities.

"It was not that this man sinned, or his parents, but that the works of God might be made manifest in him."

This answer might have seemed fatalistic until Jesus' next act. He approached the blind man and spat on the ground. He made some clay with his saliva and used it as an ointment, applying it to the blind man's eyes. After this he bid him wash himself, saying:

"Go to the pool of Siloam."

Jesus way of healing was similar in this case to the methods used by the Jewish doctors of the time, though they did not use earth and saliva and had certainly never restored sight to anyone born blind. More than a hundred people watched as the elated man jumped about and shouted, as he saw for the first time in his entire life.

This was the miracle, but there is more to say about it.

Denying the obvious

The most logical thing would have been for the family, friends and neighbours of the healed man to take part in his happiness. However, some of them hated Jesus for his attacks on the rich and for fighting against their sins, and began to say absurd things. Some said,:

"It is he," while still others said, "No, but he is like him."

The Pharisees took to this idea and maliciously went to the blind man's house to speak to his parents. They could only say:

"We know that this is our son, and that he was born blind; but how he now sees we do not know, nor do we know who opened his eyes. Ask him; he is of age, he will speak for himself."

So they went to the blind man himself:

"Give God the praise; we know that this man is a sinner."

"Whether he is a sinner, I do not know; one thing I know, that though I was blind, now I see." He saw that the Pharisees still did not believe him, so he mocked them:

"I have told you already, and you would not listen. Why do you want to hear it again? Do you too want to become his disciples?"

And they reviled him, saying, "You are his disciples, but we are disciples of Moses. We know that God has spoken to Moses, but as for this man, we do not know where he comes from."

"Why, this is a marvel! You do not know where he comes from, and yet he opened my eyes. We know that God does not listen to sinners, but if any one is a worshipper of God and does his will, God listens to him. If this man were not from God, he could do nothing."

"You were born in utter sin, and would you teach us?"

With this, the enemies left the house, 'blinder' than ever. They wanted one thing only: to prove that the man from Nazareth was an impostor. The Truth meant nothing to them in comparison to the position in society they were afraid to lose.

The reencounter with Jesus

The man who had been blind went back to the temple, this time to give thanks for being healed. Before he went in he saw a kind-looking man, who was alone and looking at him with a sweet expression. He knew immediately who he was, though he had never before set eyes on him.

"Do you believe in the Son of man?"

"And who is he, sir that I may believe in him?"

"You have seen him, and it is he who speaks to you."

And the sighted man exclaimed, "Lord, I believe," and fell to his knees.

A crowd had gathered around the two men. There were enemies there as well. Jesus directed the following words to them:

"For judgement I came into this world, that those who do not see may see, and that those who see may become blind."

"Are we also blind?" asked the Pharisees angrily.

Jesus healing the blind man

If you were blind, you would have no guilt; but now that you say, 'We see,' your guilt remains.

This was aimed directly at them, though Jesus was aware it would have no effect on them. But the humble of heart understood it perfectly.

The magic of a word

One afternoon, when Jesus and his disciples were alone, he decided to start up a game often used by the masters of the Orient.

"Who do men say that the Son of man is?" he asked.

Nobody wished to remain silent, but some answered that he was John, others, Elijah, and others, Jeremiah, always considering him a prophet. They did not pause to reflect before they answered. The Master asked them again:

"But who do you say that I am?"

His question met with silence. They seemed dumbstruck and afraid to commit themselves. Then Peter, the most impulsive of the disciples, answered:

"You are the Messiah, the Son of the Living God."

'Messiah'. It was a magic word with an infinite number of meanings. Jesus looked at Peter and seemed not to see him. Reality had turned a simple game into something obvious: there was little time left before his end.

Before he came back to himself, Jesus embraced Peter and solemnly blessed him:

"Blessed are you, Simon Bar-Jona! For flesh and blood has not revealed this to you, but my Father who is in heaven"

He had never praised any of his disciples so highly. The interesting thing is that Jesus quickly recovered his serious nature, and asked all those present to keep quiet what they had heard, and lastly, decided that they had spent much time in Galilee and should return to Jerusalem.

Those who were there were a little shaken, but not even Peter dared to remind him that they were going back into the snake's nest. It was there that the Jewish bourgeoisie had more in store for Jesus than just stones.

An increasingly prophetic message

Jesus did not stop preaching wherever he went, but his message became increasingly inscrutable and deep. It was perhaps more human than ever, even though it became very dramatic.

124

"If any man would come after me, let him deny himself and take up his cross and follow me. For whoever would save his life will lose it, and whoever loses his life for my sake will find it. For what will it profit a man, if he gains the whole world and forfeits his life? Or what shall a man give in return for his life? For the Son of Man is to come with his angels in the glory of his Father, and then he will repay every man for what he has done. Truly, I say to you, there are some standing here who will not taste death before they see the Son of Man coming in his kingdom."

Jesus was speaking like the prophets, using both promises and threats. Soon his most frequently repeated message was "He who is not with me is against me!"

This was a clear sign for those who were with him to the end. It was a bitter commitment with no going back. Jesus and his disciples were about to face a great split, and though they did not know how it would come about, they could feel that it was going to happen.

Jesus challenges his destiny

One morning, when Jesus was inside synagogue at Capernaum, surrounded by hundreds of people, he dared to present himself as the Messiah to the priest himself, who was at the front of the crowd:

"I am the bread of life; he who comes to me shall not hunger, and he who believes in me shall never thirst. For I have come down from heaven, not to do my own will, but the will of him who sent me. For this is the will of my Father, that every one who sees the Son and believes in him should have eternal life; and I will raise him up at the last day."

The Pharisees who were listening looked at each other in mutual understanding, as they had just heard yet another example of blasphemy from the son of Mary and Joseph, the humble couple from Nazareth, who eked out their living from carpentry. How had this so-called Messiah not even taken proper care of them?

The disciples became uneasy watching the reactions of their enemies. Jesus encouraged them by saying:

"Do you take offence at this? Then what if you were to see the Son of Man ascending where he was before? It is the spirit that gives life, the flesh is of no avail; the words that I have spoken to you are spirit and life. But there are some of you that do not believe."

Those who would never follow him however many miracles he managed to perform sent new reports to the Sanhedrin, and also to Herod, who had spent some months convinced that Jesus was a materialisation of John the Baptist's aggressive desires. There were many people by now who wanted the revolutionary dead.

But this was a threat that could not frighten the Messiah, for he could see what was going to happen years later.

"O Jerusalem, Jerusalem, killing the prophets and stoning those who are sent to you! How often would I have gathered your children together as a hen gathers her brood under her wings, and you would not! Behold, your house is forsaken and desolate. For I tell you, you will not see me again until you say 'Blessed is he who comes in the name of the Lord.'"

In this way he announced what was to happen very soon, when he reached to city where the greatest tragedies in Israel had 'always' occurred. The one awaiting him, however, was the most terrible of them all.

CHAPTER X

DAYS OF HALLELUJAHS AND FATEFUL SHADOWS

'King of Jerusalem!'

On a Sunday, Jesus left Bethany with his disciples and went up on the Mount of Olives. Near Bethphage, the Master said to two of the most faithful:

"Go into the village oppose you, and immediately you will find an ass tied, and a colt with her; untie them and bring them to me. If any one says anything to you, you shall say, 'The Lord has need of them,' and he will send them immediately."

He was respecting the prophecy of Zechariah that announced that the Lord's promised King would come into Jerusalem 'on a fully developed animal, the foal of an ass.' King Solomon also rode on one when he was anointed as the sovereign of Israel.

Meanwhile, the Feast of the Passover was being celebrated in Jerusalem. Never had so many people been seen in the streets and around the main gate. Stalls extended to the le and right, and rows of people moved this way and that rying branches taken from mulberry and fig trees and p by the side of the road. Thousands of loud voices, som singing, sometimes laughing, filled the streets. Peo dancing and calling to each other. It was a true fea ure and recreation, where people left behind their heavy hearts and a year of calamities...

Suddenly, about twenty Galileans appeared among the crowd, together with their wives. They were in even higher spirits. At first nobody noticed them except for people coming into the city, and soon they began to alert others.

So it was that thousands of pairs of eyes eventually came to rest on a man riding an ass. He was dressed in a white cloak which though it was covered in dust gave him an impressive, regal appearance. It was not surprising to see how the Galileans received him with hundreds of palm branches and chants such as:

"Blessed be he who comes in the name of the Lord! Hosanna in the highest!"

This hymn was known as the Great Hellel, and they sung it at the synagogue while they walked round and round the altar showing their palm leaves in honour of the son of David. The most fervent believers among the Jews became alarmed, but the voices had changed:

"Tell the daughter of Zion, Behold your king is coming to you, humble, and mounted on an ass."

Then all the criticism and laughing died away, for the Galilean's jubilation was contagious. And people had also heard that Jesus of Nazareth was coming, he who had worked many miracles. Thousands of arms thus raised branches themselves hoarse with cries of: "Blessed is the mes in the name of the Lord! Peace in heaven he highest!"

e humble

Pharisees felt offended when they saw and As Jesus went by, they shouted to him: e your disciples."

The Messiah replied, "I tell you, if these were silent, the very stones would cry out!"

The people's clamouring did not die down until well into the afternoon. A human king would never have been greeted so spontaneously.

The triumphant entry of Jesus into Jerusalem

Jesus felt very disconsolate then. Tears came to his eyes as he imagined the destruction of Jerusalem the proud nearly forty years later (in 70 AD). With his spirits still heavy with anguish, he entered the temple as he always did when he came to a city. He was immediately surrounded by blind and disabled people whom he healed with his hands and voice. They shouted their thanks:

"Hosanna to the Son of David!"

Their cry was met with the protest of one of the most important holy men: "Do you hear what these are saying?"

"Yes; have you never read, 'Out of the mouth of babes and sucklings thou hast brought perfect praise'?"

His enemies went away, and the Master continued with his teaching. When night came he decided to go back to Bethany, perhaps to spend the night at the home of Lazarus.

Time is running out

Jesus had never been so active. Much as his disciples tried to warn him of the dangers he faced near Jerusalem, he still would not stop going there.

One morning, while was walking in the woods, he felt hungry and came to a place where nature seemed to have favoured the growth of the plants and trees. He went up to a fig tree to take one of its delicious fruits. There were so many leaves it seemed that underneath them there must be fruit hidden. But he found none, and acted strangely.

"May no fruit ever come from you again!" he punished the tree.

And the fig tree dried up and stayed like that for many years. This was the first negative testimony of what Jerusalem and everything with it was to mean.

Shortly afterwards, Jesus is thought to have expelled all the merchants and traders once again from the temple, as they were profaning 'his Father's house'. Those affected went in search of the priests and immediately asked for their assistance.

Some of them proposed killing Jesus, but others thought this would be impossible as it would cause an uprising against established power. His reception on Sunday made it easy to see that the man from Nazareth could call himself King of Jerusalem if he chose. His enemies were afraid.

The challenges continue

The following morning Jesus returned to the temple. The traders were now installed nearby but were not calling their wares or carrying out sacrifices. However, the scribes were around, ready to continue the challenges they made with the Pharisees and other members of the bourgeoisie. They waited for Jesus to make a pause in his preaching to ask him perversely:

"By what authority are you doing these things, and who gave you this authority?"

The Son of Man had been waiting for this attack, and he replied with another question:

"I also will ask you a question; and if you tell me the answer, then I will tell you by what authority I do these things. The baptism of John, whence was it? From heaven or from men?

The scribes were caught between the frying pan and the fire – whichever option they chose would expose them. They eventually answered:

"We do not know."

"Neither will I tell you by what authority I do these things", responded Jesus, turning his back on them.

A short while later he told the parable of the good son and the bad son. Their father told one of them to go and work in the vineyard. "I will not," was the reply he was met with. But he regretted his answer and went to follow his father's order. The father asked the other son to do the same and he replied that he would, but in the end never went near the vineyard. Which of the two did the will of his father?

"The first," said the scribes.

"Truly, I say to you, the tax collectors and the harlots go into the kingdom of God before you. For John came to you in the way of righteousness and you did not believe him, but the tax collectors and the harlots believed him."

His people had listened to him with respect. Meanwhile his enemies watched him with a mixture of hate and satisfaction, because when he insulted them in public he was falling into the trap they had set him.

Determined to entrap him

The Pharisees and the followers of Herod Antipas thought they had found a way to cause Jesus to make a fatal mistake. Jerusalem had a Roman governor, and if they could make him speak out against established power they could get him sentenced. So they paid some young people to dress as Galileans. These young people asked him:

"Teacher, we know that you are true, and teach the way of God truthfully, and care for no man. Tell us, then, what you think. Is it lawful to pay taxes to Caesar, or not?"

"Why put me to the test, you hypocrites? Show me the money for the tax," he said, not turning from danger though he knew nothing of taxes.

The young men showed him a Roman denarius and laughed to themselves as they thought of how they had managed to anger the man they were trying to ensnare.

"Whose likeness and inscription is this?"

"Caesar's," came the reply.

"Render therefore to Caesar the things that are Caesar's, and to God the things that are God's."

This was such a skilful, sincere answer, that the tricksters must have left with their faces red with shame. But their defeat did not discourage them, as the following day in the temple at Jerusalem temple a similar scene took place. Now these men did not believe in the resurrection, and they asked the teacher the following question:

Jesus with the two young men showing him the coin of Caesar

"Teacher, Moses said, 'If a man dies, having no children, his brother must marry the widow, and raise up the children for his brother.' Now there were seven brothers among us;

133

the first married, and died, and having no children left his wife to his brother. So too the second and third, down to the seventh. After them all, the woman died. In the resurrection, therefore, to which of the seven will she be wife? For they all had her."

"You are wrong, because you know neither the scriptures nor the power of God. For in the resurrection they neither marry nor are given in marriage, but are like angels in heaven. And as for the resurrection of the dead, have you not read what was said to you by God, 'I am the God of Abraham, and the God of Isaac, and the God of Jacob'? He is not God of the dead, but of the living."

The priests and others who knew the holy books were stunned, because everything they had just heard was written there. He had the religious knowledge of a wise man. There was no way they could accuse him of blasphemy, but they continued their verbal haranguing:

"Which commandment is the first of all?"

"Hear, O Israel: You shall love the Lord your God with all your heart, and with all you soul, and with all your mind, and with all your strength.' The second is this, 'You shall love your neighbour as yourself.' There is no other commandment greater than these."

Did he want to provoke the final onslaught?

As a last option, the Pharisees went to a woman who had been arrested for adultery. They took her out of prison and brought her near to the temple, where she encountered Jesus and his disciples.

"Teacher, this woman has been caught in the act of adultery," said the leader of the group. "Now in the law Moses commanded us to stone such. What do you say about her?"

"Let him who is without sin among you be the first to throw a stone at her."

The unhappy woman was set free. Her jailers were so humiliated by Jesus' reply that they ran off, probably to set another trap.

"Woman, where are they?" asked the Son of Man. "Has no one condemned you?"

"No one, Lord."

"Neither do I condemn you; go, and do not sin again."

A difficult problem was thus calmly solved. Days later in the temple, his attitude was very different. Perhaps he wished to provoke his enemies' final attack. Among his hundreds of listeners were some of them, to whom he aimed these cutting words:

"The scribes and Pharisees sit on Moses' seat; so practice and observe whatever they tell you, but not what they do; for they preach, but do not practise. They bind heavy burdens, hard to bear, and lay them on men's shoulders; but they themselves will not move them with their finger. They do all their deeds to be seen by men; for they make their phylacteries broad and their fringes long, and they love the place of honour at feasts and the best seats in the synagogues, and salutations in the market places, and being called rabbi by men.

"But woe to you, scribes and Pharisees, hypocrites! Because you shut the kingdom of heaven against men; for you neither enter yourselves, nor allow those who would enter to go in.

"Woe to you, blind guides, who say, 'If anyone swears by the temple, it is nothing; but if any one swears by the gold of the temple, he is bound by his oath.' You blind fools! For which is greater, the gold or the temple that has made the gold sacred?

"Woe to you, scribes and Pharisees, hypocrites! For you tithe mint and dill and cumin, and have neglected the weightier matters of the law, justice and mercy and faith; these you

135

ought to have done, without neglecting the others. You blind guides, straining out a gnat and swallowing a camel!

"You cleanse the outside of the cup and of the plate, but inside they are full of extortion and rapacity. You blind Pharisee! First cleanse the inside of the cup and of the plate, that the outside also may be clean.

"You are like whitewashed tombs, which outwardly appear beautiful, but within they are full of dead men's bones and all uncleanness. So you also outwardly appear righteous to men, but within you are full of hypocrisy and iniquity.

"You build the tombs of the prophets, saying, 'If we had lived in the days of our fathers, we would not have taken part with them in shedding the blood of the prophets.' Thus you witness against yourselves, that you are sons of those who murdered the prophets. You serpents, you brood of vipers, how are you to escape being sentenced to hell?"

This counterattack was so aggressive that his persecutors thought they finally had enough evidence to incriminate him. They went quickly to the Sanhedrin, where Nicodemus and his friends could no longer do anything to stay their vengeance.

The generous widow

Jesus and his disciples were about to leave the temple when they were stopped in their tracks by a moving scene. Thirteen boxes were placed ready to receive alms. There were people gathered around them. Many men dressed in luxurious clothing were asking their slaves to fetch coins for them so that they could show off to others when they gave their donations. Meanwhile, a poor woman dressed in mourning, clean, yet many times patched, was waiting for them to make way for her so that she could give her coins, which she was hiding. She was eventually able to deposit them there. There were two silver coins. This behaviour led the Master to declare:

"Truly I tell you, this poor widow has put in more than all of them; for they all contributed out of their abundance, but she out of her poverty put in all the living that she had."

In the face of false vanity

Even though his end was growing ever nearer, Jesus' disciples seemed to be preoccupied with superfluous concerns. Sometimes they did not realise they were falling into false or useless forms of vanity.

One day, Salome, the mother of the disciples Jacob and John, demanded:

"Command that these two sons of mine may sit, one at your right hand and one at your left, in your kingdom."

"You do not know what you are asking. Are you able to drink the cup that I am to drink?"

When he saw that those concerned were nodding their heads, he added, "To sit at my right hand and at my left is not mine to grant, but it is for those for whom it has been prepared by my Father."

The next day, the disciples got into an absurd dispute, wanting to know who would be the greatest in the kingdom of heaven. Jesus must have sorted out the situation with these words:

"The kings of the Gentiles exercise lordship over them; and those in authority over them are called benefactors. But not so with you; rather let the greatest among you become as the youngest, and the leader as one who serves. For which is the greater, one who sits at table, or one who serves? Is it not the one who sits at table? But I am among you as one who serves."

It was a great show of humility, unarguable proof of the equality of all human beings. The governor and his servants were equal before God, because all social differences would disappear when moral behaviour was more important. The Truth according to Jesus seemed very simple, but his disciples would need to see him die on the cross to truly understand it. Meanwhile, small vanities continued to occupy their minds. And in one exceptional case, this would lead to the worst of betrayals...

Jesus was the divine judge

One afternoon in Bethany, Jesus spoke as energetically as in earlier times to his disciples after eating.

"They will see the Son of man coming in clouds with great power and glory. And then he will send out the angels, and gather the elect from the four winds, from the ends of the earth to the ends of heaven. Truly, I say to you, this generation will not pass away before all these things take place. Heaven and earth will pass away, but my words will not pass away.

"When the Son of Man comes in his glory, and all the angels with him, then he will sit on his glorious throne. Before him will be gathered all the nations, and he will separate them one from another as a shepherd separates the sheep from the goats, and he will place the sheep at his right hand, but the goats at the left. Then the King will say to those at his right hand, 'Come, O blessed of my Father, inherit the kingdom prepared for you from the foundation of the world; for I was hungry and you gave me food, I was thirsty and you gave me drink. Truly, I say to you, as you did it to one of the least of these my brethren, you did it to me.'"

He had just shown himself to be a fair, impartial divine judge. All of those around him believed him, except for one, Judas, who had been doubting for five days, ever since they had reached Jerusalem.

CHAPTER XI

TIMES OF INFINITE ANGUISH

A perfumed balsam for the Messiah

Suddenly a very beautiful woman appeared. Some thought she was like Mary Magdalene while she was working as a prostitute, and so they did not throw her out. They trusted that Jesus would make this decision. What she wanted was to approach the true Messiah. She went up to him, took out a flask of perfume, and poured its contents over his head to anoint him.

All present watched the scene and were moved by it. Only Judas got up to criticise it:

"Why was the ointment thus wasted? For this ointment might have been sold for more than three hundred denarii, and given to the poor."

No confrontation like this had ever been heard between Jesus and any of his disciples. Jesus and Judas looked at each other as if all links between them had just been broken, but the wiser man stayed calm, while Judas became uneasy, realising he had gone too far. He was sweetly reproached for his conduct by Jesus.

"Let her alone; why do you trouble her? She has done a beautiful thing to me. For you always have the poor with you, but you will not always have me. She has done what she could; she has anointed my body beforehand for burying." He turned towards her and said in voice full of emotion, "And truly, I say to you, wherever the gospel is preached in the whole world, what she has done will be told in memory of her."

Judas or 'the one who had lived'

Much has been written about Judas. Now we know he was the oldest and most experienced of the disciples, one of the last to join Jesus. He was from the bourgeoisie, had had relations with several women, had lived comfortably and committed several sins of covetousness, lust and lack of mercy. These were mistakes the other disciples had also made and for which they had been forgiven through sincere repentance.

It is thought that Judas followed Jesus because he was fascinated by his way of speaking, the marvels he did and the pure image he gave off. We might sum this up by saying it was Judas' impossible dream. He was caught up in his spell in Galilee, where he had gone to escape from his previous life, perhaps through frustration.

This frustration wore off over time. When Judas was in Jerusalem, which was where he had been brought up, the pleasures of the city and the promises of his old friends led him into betrayal.

Some have chosen to see in his acts a feeling of spite because his decisions regarding the use of the common funds were not being respected. But this reason does not seem very substantial to us, as we are more inclined to favour the previous one, which was that he slowly began to feel more inclined towards the Pharisees than Jesus and his followers.

Thirty coins for Jesus

Jesus' enemies had run out of tactics. All the members of the Sanhedrin met to talk about how they could find a way to get rid of the revolutionary. On the following day, the week of the Passover Feast would come to an end and if the people of Jerusalem continued to hear so many insults against those in power they might rise up in arms. This had to be prevented regardless of what it took. But how?

Suddenly one of the priests was informed that a friend of his, who called himself Judas Iscariot, wished to be received by the Sanhedrin. He could not contain his victory cry.

"Here is the man who is going to hand Jesus over to us! He is one of his disciples!"

The traitor entered with a show of assurance, stood in the middle of the room and in a cruel voice asked:

Judas selling Jesus for a few pieces of silver

"What will you give me if I deliver him to you?"

"Thirty pieces of silver," said the most astute of the judges, who knew a spiteful betrayal when he saw one.

While the bag of money was being handed over, all the members of the Sanhedrin, except for Nicodemus and his allies, congratulated themselves. Being given the chance to arrest the man from Nazareth because of the betrayal of one of his disciples was the final incriminatory evidence.

So the prophetic psalm came true: "Even my bosom friend in whom I trusted, who ate of my bread, has lifted his heel against me."

The beginning of the Last Supper

Jesus was ready to hold the feast of Unleavened Bread. This was always done to commemorate the saving of first-born children when the Jewish people were held captive in Egypt. Because they would all be together in a house in Jerusalem, all possible precautions were taken.

Here, we will make use of a perfect image of what was to happen, following the text of Jean-Paul Roux taken from his work *Jesus of Nazareth*:

When night fell and all was made ready, Jesus came to the table with the Twelve and said to them, "I have earnestly desired to eat this Passover with you before I suffer; for I tell you I shall not eat it until it is fulfilled in the kingdom of God..." And, taking the chalice that was ritually used to start meals, he drank from it and wet his lips on it, and gave it to his disciples, saying, "Take this, and divide it among yourselves; for I tell you that from now on I shall not drink of the fruit of the vine until the kingdom of God comes." The celestial beatitude the psalms had spoken of in terrible, mysterious words was for this cup of life in which drops of water were mixed: "My cup runneth over," sung the world over by mystics. Would Jesus never again drink from the cup of fortune? He would suffer to the end of time at the altar of the mass, this, his constantly renewed sacrifice.

The established custom was to wash one's hands before eating, although to protest against legalism, the disciples often respect this formality. This infraction was even more evident in the foot washing ceremony. Of course, behind this ceremony is the symbolism of the foot and specifically the powerful idea of the foot leaving its tracks behind along the path, good or bad, that it has chosen, and also that it carries the marks, as shoes carry the mud or dust of paths, the sign of the places it has travelled through. The water that is poured over it carries away, together with the signs it has left, all the impure actions of men. However, as Jesus explained, the moral lesson seems more important here. Wishing to humble himself before the apostles, to teach them that the greatest must serve the most humble (the very fundament of any monarchy), Jesus put aside his garments and, girding himself with a towel, poured water into a basin as a slave would have done, and began to wash the feet of all of his disciples and to dry them with the towel he wore about his waist.

They fell silent, stunned. But impetuous Peter, who was not given to mysticism, exclaimed:

"Lord, do you wash my feet?"

Jesus answered: "What I am doing you do not know now, but afterward you will understand."

Peter said, "You shall never wash my feet," and Jesus answered: "If I do not wash you, you have not part in me..."

Simon Peter then replied, "Lord, not my feet only but also my hands and my head!" And Jesus answered, "He who has bathed does not need to wash, except for his feet, but he is clean all over; and you are clean, but not every one of you."

143

When he had finished, he took his clothes and sat down again at the table. They started to eat.

Jesus had said, "You are clean, but not every one of you." He felt disturbed at the thought of Judas' betrayal. He said to them: "Truly I say to you, one of you will betray me,." The disciples looked at each other without knowing whom he was talking about.

Judas, signalled by Jesus

The table where they ate the Last Supper was so low that all the disciples could eat sitting on the floor. The banquet was normally accompanied by bitter herbs and afterwards, *kharoset* (stewed fruit) was eaten. The table was always blessed. Then the food was removed from the table and the guests would share a glass of watered wine between them. Finally, the table was laid again and the unleavened bread was brought.

Jesus took one piece, broke it, and said:

"Praise be to he who makes the bread grow out of the ground!"

Next he wrapped the bread in bitter herbs, dipped it into the *kharoset* and ate it. Then he prayed again. The Passover lamb was brought to the table. While the disciples were reaching for the meat, the Messiah said:

He who has dipped his hand in the dish with me, will betray me. The Son of man goes as it is written of him, but woe to that man by whom the Son of man is betrayed! It would have been better for that man if he had not been born."

A shiver of fear went through the disciples, but Judas was the most affected. The innocent among them asked him: "*Is it I, Master?*"

When Judas asked this in a whisper, Jesus answered him: *"You have said so."*

Then John, whose head was lying on the Master's chest, asked: *"Lord, who is it?"*

"It is he to whom I shall give this morsel when I have dipped it."

He dipped a piece of bread into the wine and gave it straight to Judas, saying:

"What you are going to do, do quickly."

The Last Supper

Here it is to be taken that the other eleven disciples did not realise what had just happened, as it is impossible to believe that they did not jump onto the traitor in anger. Perhaps the last dialogue was whispered and the others did not hear it. Whatever the case may have been, Judas left quickly.

The first Eucharist

If we take the four official Gospels as our evidence it is difficult to discern when the Eucharist was actually formalised during the Last Supper. We imagine it to have taken place after Judas' escape.

Jesus took bread, gave thanks and broke it, and gave it to his disciples, as he said in the gentlest of voices: "Take and eat; this is my body."

Then after supper he took the cup, gave thanks, and gave it to all to drink, saying,

"This cup is the new covenant in my blood. Do this, as often as you drink it, in remembrance of me. For as often as you eat this bread and drink the cup, you proclaim the Lord's death until he comes."

Next Jesus shared the wine or 'blood' out among all his disciples. Thus the Eucharist was brought in.

The walk on the Mount of Olives

The night was full of the noise and smell of feasts. The Passover was being celebrated inside peoples' homes in Jerusalem. The Mount of Olives was therefore deserted and it offered a peaceful place to those who needed it. Jesus and his disciples went up silently, shaken. Another transfiguration was taking place: The face of the Master had gone pale, his eyes were raised to heaven and a controlled shaking made

146

him walk almost rigidly. Drops of sweat appeared on his forehead.

Before they could ask him what was wrong, though, he came back to himself and with a grave expression on his face, asked:

"When I sent you out with no purse or bag or sandals, did you lack anything?"

"Nothing, Master," they answered together.

"But now, let him who has a purse take it, and likewise a bag. And let him who has no sword sell his mantle and buy one." This idea left them all amazed, as if they had been taken by surprise wondering if it was not time they carried arms with them. Two of them were already doing so and they said to him spiritedly:

"Look, Lord, here are two swords."

Jesus immediately realised his mistake, for he had been consumed by a last desire to resist, when there was now no way of changing the course of his destiny. And in the sweetest voice he could manage he advised them:

"Let us forget violence." The only thing he cared about now was the future of his disciples and he forewarned them: "You will all fall away because of me this night; for it is written, 'I will strike the shepherd, and the sheep of the flock will be scattered.'"

On hearing this Peter impulsively came forward and interrupted him:

"Though they all fall away because of you, I will never fall away."

"Truly, I say to you, this very night, before the cock crows, you will deny me three times."

"Even if I must die with you, I will not deny you," exclaimed Peter firmly.

The other disciples made the same promise. However, as they threaded their way up the hill in the dark, through bushes

147

and trees, Jesus had only to ask to be left alone, and they did so. He said to them:

"My soul is very sorrowful, even to death; remain here and watch with me."

The anguish of the inevitable

Jesus took a few steps forward, knelt down and pressed his forehead to the ground, and in his loneliness said:

"My Father, if it be possible, let this cup pass from me; nevertheless, not as I will, but as thou wilt."

This was the call of a man who was vulnerable to martyrdom, a man foreseeing his pain. Shock was running through his body, the veins on his neck were swollen to bursting and his forehead beaded with sweat, perhaps even blood. He showed no sign of rebellion, but rather supreme obedience to his Father.

Slowly, his responsibility gave him strength of spirit. He got up, overcome by the anguish of the inevitable, left his brief refuge and went to find his three chosen disciples. He found them asleep. Had his suffering, which seemed so short to him, lasted for hours?

He went past John and Jacob and woke up Peter, whom he reproached:

"So, could you not watch with me one hour?"

Shortly the sounds of footsteps and weapons were heard. Through the bushes shone torches, and fires burned. Jesus realised what was about to happen. He walked forward about twenty steps and this was enough. The night was dark and his disciples were asleep, for Peter did not wake up completely when he called him, and so they were in no danger.

The kiss of Judas

Judas was walking at the head of a group armed with sticks, spears and a few swords. The men had been recruited quickly, taken out of their beds for an urgent mission. They were servers of the Sanhedrin, people who never would have been able to find Jesus had they not been with someone who knew him, as well as his and his disciples' customs.

To make the moment even worse, the traitor had arranged to give the following sign: greeting Jesus with a kiss and calling him Master, allowing those who were with him to capture him faster. And so it was that he acted out the macabre farce, kissing Jesus' cheek and saying: "Hail, Master!"

Jesus and his disciples on the Mount of Olives
(drawing by Rembrandt)

Jesus' reaction was extraordinary, as he asked without any sign of bitterness:

"Friend, why are you here?"

When he called Judas 'friend', the whole patrol was overcome with unease. The captain froze with his sword held high, while Judas went as white as a corpse, shaking with regret. He looked as if he wanted to die, because he had just handed over an innocent man.

There were a few minutes of indecision, and Peter interrupted with his habitual zest and lack of reflection, more out of instinct than intelligence. Trying to save Jesus, he jumped on one of the soldiers and cut off his ear with a blow of the sword. Howls of pain caused the other armed men to react. The Son of Man was immediately arrested, while Peter fled into the shadows of the night.

Some of the members of the patrol were up in arms as they searched for the aggressor, but Jesus said to them with the integrity of someone who has fully accepted his fate:

"Put your sword back into its place; for all who take the sword will perish by the sword."

The threat was so firmly spoken that they listened to him. Much later, they took heed again of his wise words:

"Do you think that I cannot appeal to my Father, and he will at once send me more than twelve legions of angels? But how then should the scriptures be fulfilled, that it must be so? Have you come out as against a robber, with swords and clubs to capture me? Day after day I sat in the temple teaching, and you did not seize me."

Nobody knew how to answer him, for they did not understand him. He was taken from the Mount of Olives. The disciples were awake by then, yet none of them went to help their Master.

CHAPTER XII

THE SHOW OF THE PASSION

At the mercy of a bitter old man

Jesus was taken to the Sanhedrin, a true insult of a palace, full of tapestries, marble, gold and other riches. This was not proper for judge-priests who were considered the servants of the Jewish people. The most powerful of them was the old man Annas, a sort of mummy past his hundredth year, but who possessed the intelligence of a patriarch who had successively made each of his five sons High Priest, and in doing so keeping the supreme religious authority well under his control. At the time his 'heir' was Caiaphas, a true puppet in his father's hands, even though he was seventy years old and had been nominated by the Roman rulers.

A meeting of the Sanhedrin had been called, which a third of its members attended. It was enough to hold a high trial. But Nicodemus and other allies of Jesus were missing, perhaps because Judas had also betrayed them. As with the troop who arrested the man from Nazareth, it was necessary to go round the judges' houses one by one to find them and get them out of their beds after the Passover Feast.

First, a large group of witnesses was made to file before the judges, all of whom tried to prove that they had heard and seen the blasphemies spoken by Jesus of Nazareth. Once the procession of false witnesses had ended, Annas tried to get 'the accused' to speak, demanding him to explain his doctrine.

"I have spoken before the people of Israel, in the temple, in the streets, in the squares and on the mounts, said the Son of Man coldly. I have always spoken to the Jews in public, hiding nothing. Why do you interrogate me thus? Ask those who have heard me outside Jerusalem. They will tell you the truth..."

Jesus was struck suddenly, and the servant who had slapped him exclaimed:

"How dare you answer the High Priest with such arrogance?"

"If I seem arrogant," said the Messiah, ignoring the slap, "you should prove it. And if I have not the right to speak, how could you not warn me that I would be struck if I did?"

After this he kept silent for a long time, taking no notice of the demands of Annas, Caiaphas and the rest of the judges. All of them wished to hold a trial with the trappings of legality. They asked the scribes to turn a blind eye to the slap, for they wished the rebel's confession to be made "within a legal framework". It was the old man who finally came up with the key question, knowing that the man from Nazareth would not be able to silence himself.

"If you are the Christ, tell us."

Jesus realised that he would have to identify himself before his enemies so that his destiny would be prolonged no further.

"If I tell you, you will not believe; and if I ask you, you will not answer."

"I adjure you by the living God, tell us if you are the Christ, the Son of God," shouted Annas, almost standing and pointing with his scabby fingers at the victim.

152

"You have said so," said Jesus. "But I tell you, hereafter you will see the Son of man seated at the right hand of the Power, and coming on the clouds of heaven."

"He has uttered blasphemy. Why do we still need witnesses? What is your judgement?"

"He deserves death," replied all the judges.

Peter's first denial

Peter's denial

Peter was the only one of the disciples who went into Jerusalem to find out what had happened to the Master. He came to the great court of the Sanhedrin, where some of the men who had been on the Mount of Olives were gathered. He stood in the shadows out of danger to listen. But he did not realise that a woman coming out of a nearby doorway was looking at him, and shouted:

"You also were with Jesus the Galilean."

But Peter denied it, saying, "I do not know what you mean."

But one of the men took a torch and brought it up to the disciple's face. He asked him:

"This man was with Jesus of Nazareth."

And again Peter denied it: "I do not know the man."

A second server of the judge-priests stood up to second the others' accusations.

"Certainly you are also one of them, for your accent betrays you."

"I do not know the man," screamed Peter in anger, thus fooling his challengers.

They let him go. However, as he was about to walk through the door of the great courtyard, he heard the cock crow. Then he remembered Jesus' words and his cowardice made him weep bitterly.

This tragic incident took place at the same time as the reading of the sentence of the High Council. Jesus of Nazareth was sentenced to death. Hours later, the Council of Seventy went towards the Tower of Antonia with the condemned man in their midst. There they awaited the decision of Pilate, the Roman governor.

Judas commits suicide

When Judas heard himself called 'friend' by Jesus after handing him over, he was seized with regret. He wandered for hours around the Mount of Olives, the outskirts of Jerusalem and inside the city. Finally he decided to return the bag with the thirty silver coins in it. He handed it over to the priests and tried desperately to recant his accusations, shouting:

"I have sinned in betraying innocent blood!"

"What is that to us? See to it yourself," they laughed.

The traitor threw the bag to the temple floor and ran out in desperation. He found a rope along the way and went and hanged himself. Legend portrays him as a monstrous puppet, and many are the stories told of his end.

Meanwhile, the priests were facing the minor problem of what to do with the bag of coins. It was considered to be impure money, having been used to price the blood of a man, and so it could not be kept in the temple treasury. After a long discussion, it was decided to buy the potter's field, where a cemetery for strangers would be placed. This was called *Haceldama* (the Field of Blood) and it was left open for many years. Thus was fulfilled what the prophet Jeremiah had said:

"And they took the thirty pieces of silver, the price of him on whom a price had been set by some of the sons of Israel."

A tremendous farce

Pilate was more of a politician than a soldier. He did not like Jews and only came to Jerusalem during the celebrations. His position as a Roman governor made this an obligation he could not avoid, but in truth he felt outcast as he had been sent to one of the worst colonies. He also had to act out certain situations that he found repugnant, even though he him-

155

self had authorised them, such as receiving the High Priest and the judges on a raised wooden platform before the governmental palace, because it was forbidden to Jews to go into Gentile homes during the Passover and other celebrations in Israel.

"What do you accuse this man of?" he asked when Jesus was before him, with Caiaphas and other judges and soldiers.

"We found this man perverting our nation, and forbidding us to pay tribute to Caesar" shouted some of the crowd.

The High Priest raised his hand to silence them before briefly summing up the accusation:

"He says he is Christ, King of the Jews!"

This had come out of Annas' diabolical mind, to leave religious sins aside, which a pagan would consider a minor offence, and give more importance to the political side of Jesus' works. Israel was a Roman colony where several kings were under submission. The appearance of anyone else attributing this title to himself would be considered extremely dangerous. This was why they left Jesus at the mercy of Roman law.

"Are you the King of the Jews?" asked Pilate.

"Do you say this of your own accord, or did others say it to you about me?" asked the Son of Man in a friendly voice, for he had just been left alone with the governor.

"Am I a Jew?" joked the governor, but immediately took on the airs of a judge. "Your own nation and the chief priests have handed you over to me; what have you done?"

"My kingship is not of this world," spoke Jesus, as if he were preaching in Galilee. "If my kingship were of this world, my servants would fight, that I might not be handed over to the Jews."

"So you are a king?" insisted Pilate, thinking he was dealing with a dreamer.

156

"You say that I am a king. For this I was born, and for this I have come into the world, to bear witness to the truth. Everyone who is of the truth hears my voice."

"What is truth?" asked the Roman, not disguising his dislike of philosophy.

The two men stared at each other. There was so much goodness in the eyes of the accused man that Pilate must have seen it. Thinking of this he left the room and went out to where Caiaphas was waiting for him.

"I find no crime in him."

The voices of the priests rang out:

"He stirs up the people, teaching throughout all Judea, from Galilee even to this place."

"They are speaking of Galilee," said Pilate, relieved at having found a way to shirk his responsibility. "The case you have brought to me belongs to the jurisdiction of Herod Antipas. The final word will be his!"

Thus the second act of the farce had just come to its end. The third act of this great tragedy was about to begin.

The murderer of John the Baptist

More than hate, Herod Antipas had great fear of Jesus. He was in Jerusalem for political reasons and because he needed to occupy his time in some way. He thought the Passover feasts would rid him of his insomnia, for he had been having nightmares ever since he had ordered John the Baptist to be beheaded.

When he saw that he was responsible for the fate of the man from Nazareth, he tried to dodge this responsibility. But Annas pressured him, threatening not to support him in the future, and he was forced to take it on.

When Jesus was before him he asked for the accusations against him to be read out and then gave him a chance to defend himself. But the accused refused to say even one word to the man who had murdered John. It was this silence which ended the third act of the farce.

Something peculiar occurred, however. Pilate's wife had seen Jesus and he had reminded her of the noble thinkers of Rome and Alexandria she had conversed with. Feeling great pity for him, she ran to her husband and tried to get her way by lying to him:

"Have nothing to do with that righteous man, for I have suffered much over him today in a dream."

Barabbas is chosen

Pilate was sure of Jesus' innocence and he said so to Caiaphas, the High Priest:

"I did not find this man guilty of any of your charges against him; neither did Herod. I will therefore chastise him and release him."

But the old man Annas had foreseen this outcome. He cunningly used his knowledge of the traditions of Jerusalem to make use of the Roman obligation to set free a Jewish prisoner and thus celebrate the liberation of Israel. This gesture was meant to lessen the servitude of the subjugated people. A huge crowd came to the governor's palace to demand their right:

"It is Passover; release one man!"

The smug members of the Sanhedrin continued shouting until the governor came out to attend to them. He conveniently offered to set free the King of the Jews.

The people said nothing, unsure exactly of what was being asked of them. The priests began to doubt, but Caiaphas knew what he was doing. One of his followers was among the crowd and it was he who shouted: "Release Barabbas!"

Barabbas was a follower of Judas the Zealot, who had confronted the Roman guard together with a group of Galilean rebels the previous autumn. The priests repeated the jailed man's name so enthusiastically that soon their voices were echoed by the masses, who clamoured:

"Release Barabbas!"

Pilate could not believe his eyes and ears. They wanted to save a man who had committed blood crimes while they condemned an innocent man. To free his conscience, he made another offer to the people of Jerusalem:

"Then what shall I do with the man whom you call the King of the Jews?

The crown of thorns (drawing by Rembrandt)

The voice that had to keep the spark of cruelty alive in the crowd intervened in Annas' name:

"Crucify him!"

And the unthinking mass, so easily manipulated with a few agitators in it, followed:

"Crucify him!"

A crown of thorns

Pilate was shocked in disbelief. He raised his hands to ask for silence and asked:

"What evil has he done?"

The serpent among them was cunning and well trained. He was able to answer as Annas would have done:

"If you release this man, you are not Caesar's friend; every one who makes himself a king sets himself against Caesar."

Pilate found himself with his back against the wall but still thought there might be a chance of saving the innocent man. He went back inside and gave orders for the prisoner to be tortured. He left him at the soldiers' mercy.

The soldiers had been trained to sow panic wherever they went. How could a garrison of a few Romans dominate a population of tens of thousands of people if they treated them indulgently?

First, they took off the white cloak Herod had ordered to be put on Jesus to ridicule him. Once his back was naked they tied him to a column of the courtyard and brutally whipped him with an iron chain with flecks made of small bones and lead balls, stripping the skin. The martyred man did not cry out even once, though he did moan as he tried to contain his pain.

When his torturers' arms got tired they dressed him as a king, in a worn military cape that stuck to his flesh and was soon soaked with his blood; a worm-eaten cane as a sceptre;

160

and a crown of thorns made from a garden hedge. They placed this around his head and the blood that flowed from his forehead bathed his entire face and the upper part of his body.

Jesus was taken before the crowd in this pathetic state, held up by the soldiers as he could no longer stand up alone. Pilate thought that now he would be able to save him, but he had made a serious mistake and soon realised it. The crowd laughed out loud, urged on by the priests.

"Behold the man!" shouted Pilate. "What should I do with him?"

"Crucify him! Crucify him!" shouted the maddened crowds.

"Take him and crucify him yourselves," said the Roman governor, defeated.

To give further evidence of his humiliation, he asked for a bowl, and in front of the High Priest and Jesus himself, washed his hands. As he dried them he said:

"I am innocent of this man's blood; see to it yourselves."

The long road to Golgotha

The crucifixion was prepared. Two other sentenced men were taken out of jail to be executed with Jesus. Three centurions headed the group, which was made up of two or three dozen soldiers. Food rations were prepared for the men who would spend the night guarding the crosses and finally the victim was sent for.

Meanwhile, Annas and Caiaphas thought about how they could watch over the cross in case any of his followers decided to incite the masses to action. They decided to control the situation for as long as they could and ordered some priests to cover the entire area. In this way any rumours of rebellion could be aborted.

The uphill slope that led from the prison to Golgotha was about a thousand Roman paces long (about three thousand

161

feet). It was a torment for a bleeding man who had to carry his cross as he walked. He had to go through the city centre as the law demanded, for sentenced men were used to 'set an example' to others who might commit crimes.

The sky over Jerusalem was completely clear, a burning sun beat down, and the people stirred by the side of the pathway, wishing to contemplate the scene. The traders were also there with their stalls, as the Passover was not yet over.

Ahead of the group, soldiers on horseback cleared a pathway through the crowd. Trumpets announced the arrival of the dismal party. For a while along the way Jesus was helped to carry his cross by Simon of Cyrene. He also saw his mother Mary, Mary Magdalene, and other woman whom he managed to speak to. One of them, called Veronica, cleaned his face with a cloth on which an almost exact imprint was left of his face.

It was a long path, and seemed almost never-ending to Jesus, whose strength was failing. Few writers have managed to evoke it as well as José Luis Martín Descalzo in his book *"Jesús de Nazaret"*:

The third station

In the middle was Jesus, suffocated by the weight of the cross that crushed his lungs, already hurt by the blows. There were moments when he nearly lost consciousness. The walls of the houses and the faces of the howling masses danced before his eyes. He heard their shouts but could not understand them. Sometimes he thought he was hearing a Galilean accent and for seconds, images filled his head: the sweet lake of his village, his mother, his people hearing his words on the mount. All of it seemed so far away. Now all that was before him was the horizon of death that terrified him as it would any human being. He loved life. He felt good on the Earth of mankind. He loved everything around him: the sun, water, the company of others. But all of this was fading away. His life as a man had finished. In a few hours he would no longer have to drink from this cup of pain and his head would finally come to rest on his pained chest. He wished it all could have ended some other way. But he knew there was no other.

The cruel road to Golgotha

The sins of the world had closed off all other paths. In truth, this horizon had been present throughout his lifetime and stopped him from fully enjoying humanity. He had been

163

made a man for this. But he perhaps hoped for the fruits of his life to be a little more visible; someone who would help him in this hour when he was surrounded by accusers. He was desolately alone. He felt that so much pain would have been for nothing. And this loneliness was the bitterest drop of the cup from which he drank.

This anguish weakened him even more than the lashes of the whip. He began to lose consciousness again. He felt as though his feet were floating, and could not feel the ground they stood on. He heard the centurion shout for him to carry on. And he saw faces and suns and horses and spears and dancing traders. He saw the floor rise up to meet his face and fell onto his shoulder, feeling a burning in his right knee, and was unconscious for a few seconds until he was woken by the rope that pulled on his waist...

Jesus was a man and went through the worst sufferings as a man, getting ever closer to his death. The worst thing was that he could not help but ask himself "Will all this have been worth it?" A remote hope encouraged him to bear it, but doubt often came to the forefront... "How could he convince the world to believe him if he was giving up his life for having defended the Truth?"

CHAPTER XIII

THE MYSTERY OF JESUS' DEATH

A fine literary figure

Jesus' three years of activism were full of miracles, the proof of his enormous goodness, the thousands of words he had spoken, leaving his condition as the Son of God clear. But he was sold by one of his own men, arrested, and found no one to defend him from ending up on the hill. He was crucified with two robbers, and the only people there to keep him company in silence were several women.

In his gospel, St. Matthew offers us the following regarding the hour in which Christ died: "Now from the sixth hour there was darkness over all the land until the ninth hour." No more effective figure of speech could be found here. It gives us the idea that Yahweh covered the whole area in darkness to show the immense pain the death of his Son gave him, and it must have made the men who murdered him feel the weight of their terrible crime as the lack of light sent a shiver through them.

The other gospels do not mention the darkness, but we would like to centre on them briefly as a circumstance that can be used to prove the historical truth of the event. We must remember that Jesus' existence has not been archaeologically proven.

The sixth hour is our midday, and the ninth hour is three in the afternoon. During this time in Palestine the sun would have shone strongly, but everything was covered in a thick blanket of darkness, darker than night. Some historians have speculated that this could have been a solar eclipse, which would explain these shadows as being as black as the thickest darkness.

However, this phenomenon must be excluded. The Crucifixion took place on the last day of the Passover, which always coincided with the full moon. Any amateur meteorologist knows that during a full moon, only lunar eclipses can take place, never solar ones.

Another frequently expounded hypothesis is that a great sandstorm swept the area. This could never have had such an effect, for these were frequent phenomena and just barely obscured the Sun or Moon, whose light became tinted with red through the veil of the storm, but there was never true darkness. This explanation is thus incorrect.

The date given by Juan Malalas

Richard Henning, in his book, *Great enigmas of the Universe*, writes:

Something needs to be said as to the true date of Jesus Christ's death, for the correct date must be used in astronomy if a calculable phenomenon of celestial activity is to be proven. During the years that we can consider to have been the public life of Jesus – from 29 to 33 AD – the Passover Feast only fell twice on the Saturday after the Friday of Crucifixion, and so serious attention has only been given to two years: the Passover celebrations of April 8th, 30 AD of the Roman calendar, and those of April 4th, 33 AD; both of these coincided with the Jewish Sabbath and were thus considered 'great Sabbaths'. Thus, the day of his death could only have been April 7th of the year 30 AD or April 3rd, 33

AD. All historians seem to agree on this point. However, which of these days is the true one is still a matter of debate, as both have had their defenders and critics. But the scales seem to lean in favour of the year 33. Baron Bedeus in particular has given good reasons for this. The question can be resolved beyond all doubt if the following two points of view are taken into account: firstly, the fact that a later Christian indicated, possibly basing the evidence on lost traditions, that Christ was crucified at the time of the Sulla and Sulpicius; secondly, that on April 3rd a darkening of the earth did actually take place in Jerusalem, a lunar eclipse. Both factors make it possible to definitively situate the crucifixion of Christ on April 3rd, 33 AD.

The aforementioned Christian writer is Juan Malalas, who lived in the fifth century and whose chronological exactitude in his work is noteworthy. He mentions, amongst other things, the Antiochian Era, very rarely quoted and only known about in Antioch; and this leads us to believe that he was basing his words on an ancient tradition that originated there. Malalas writes as follows:

"In the eighteenth year and seventh month of the reign of the Emperor Tiberius, Jesus Christ, our Saviour, was betrayed, at thirty three years of age, by his disciple Judas Iscariot. Our Lord Jesus Christ was crucified on the seventh day before the first day of April, in the month of March, on the fourteenth day of the moon... in times of the consulate of Sulla and Sulpicius, in the year 79 of the Antiochian Era, when Cassius was governor of Syria, named proconsul of this country by the Emperor Tiberius."

Here we have to consider that the day of Jesus Christ's death is quoted as March 25th, only because this was the date of the spring equinox at the time, just as the date of Christ's birth was stated as being the year 29, a year which cannot then be considered to be that of his death. And it was never

167

the 14th of the month of Nisan ("on the fourteenth day of the moon"). As for the rest of Juan Malalas' account, it is extremely important. The years of Emperor Tiberius' reign were counted from September 17th, 14AD, and therefore the seventh month of the nineteenth year of his rule would fall precisely from March 17th to April 16th, 33 AD, and this possibility is heightened by the naming of the consuls who at the time were actually Servius Sulpicius Galba (later Emperor Galba) and L. Cornelius Sulla Felix. However, no proconsul of Syria is known by the name of Cassius, though it is possible that he ruled for a short time, after the proconsul Aelius Lamia, whose rule finished in the year 32, and before the proconsul L. Pomponius Flaccus came to power and was sent to Syria until 35 AD. But this point is irrelevant.

The information given by Juan Malalas is enough to fix the date of Jesus' death as the year 33 AD, and this has been supported by the Baron Bedeus with weighty arguments. The main defender of the year 30 as the death of Jesus Christ is Oswald Gerhardt, who has not given any convincing arguments to support his thesis. All the reasons he has given have been proven false.

If we can then pinpoint April 3rd, 33 AD with almost complete security as the day Jesus Christ died, then the darkness mentioned in the Gospel can also be accounted for. Astronomers calculate that there was a total lunar eclipse on that day in Jerusalem, not a solar one. It began at 17:44 local time, before the moon had actually come out... and there was partial darkness until 18:37. One can understand how those who witnessed the tragedy on Golgotha were profoundly moved by the sight of the moon disappearing behind a veil of darkness, as if in mourning, and the words of the Roman centurion, "Truly, this is the Son of God," probably expressed the impression of all those present at this emotional event, the only one of its kind in the History of the world...

The crucifixion (drawing by Rembrandt)

The sublime moment of the Passion

Any novelist would give anything to come up with a plot like that of the Passion, with its ending so tragic it must be considered sublime, not just because it is Jesus Christ who is portrayed, in his condition as a Man who has not lost his identity as the Son of God. After having been through so much humiliation, with his wrists torn by two enormous nails, his arms spread wide, his face dripping with blood from the thorns

169

around his head, thirsty and hungry, he raised his head to the sky and whispered:

"Forgive them, Father, for they know not what they do."

Just then a soldier soaked a sponge in vinegar and spiked it on a spear, raising it to wet the lips of the man condemned to the worst of all deaths. Jesus had been on the cross from the sixth hour and died on it in the ninth hour. But before dying he spoke the following words. Of the four evangelists, only Matthew and Mark mention this:

"My God, my God, why hast thou forsaken me?"

Yet it is Luke who writes that Jesus words were, "Father, into thy hands I commit my spirit."

John, meanwhile, mentions other words:

"It is finished."

If we take as our premise that the four gospels complement each other, we come across an obvious contradiction here. The first phrases can be understood as the laments of a dying man on the verge of desperation, who reproaches God for letting him die in such painful circumstances, after being submitted to a trial that he was almost unable to bear, while the other two show resignation, as well as trust and a sort of consolation that the Passion was coming to its end after such suffering.

There is also another very interesting moment during the last hours of the life of Jesus Christ, concerning the spear that the Roman centurion pierces his side with. It seems like a merciful gesture with a view to hurrying the victim's death to spare him further pain. However, this is not the true reason for the act, as it was common practice to do this to victims of crucifixion.

The Gospels do not agree, either, as to the time at which Christ died. If we heed all the information given, we find that he hung from the cross for about six hours. The most logical thing would be to opt for an average time given by doctors of three hours.

What happened afterwards?

We have already mentioned the darkness that accompanied the death of Jesus. It was an unexpected circumstance, a lunar eclipse or a fog that came out of the Dead Sea and filled all those present with fear. Many of them understood that an enormous injustice had been committed and the heavens themselves were protesting.

The Sabbath was about to begin, with the celebration of Passover, and therefore the victims could not remain on their crosses. Before the three men died (Jesus and the two thieves), the priests ordered their legs to be broken to end their lives as soon as possible. This was done to the two robbers, but Jesus was speared in the side, and water and blood ran from his wound.

It is surprising that Jesus' legs were not broken; also, that Joseph of Arimathea was authorised to take down his body from the cross and remove it to a new tomb that had been opened in the rock and seal it with a stone.

Joseph of Arimathea is mentioned in all four gospels. He moved the body after obtaining Pilate's permission. At this moment, he enters into the legend, for he is said to have carried the Holy Grail, the cup from the last supper. It is said to have protected him throughout the long time he spent in prison, and then later through a journey to the very edges of Europe. He arrived in the city of Glastonbury in the south east of Great Britain, where the monks fed the myth, and it became linked to King Arthur and the Round Table. But there is also a chance it ended up in the Pyrenees in a cave, or perhaps in Italy.

What if Jesus was not truly dead?

Many very interesting books have been published speculating that Jesus did not truly die. Some writers such as Kurt

Berna base their hypothesis on the Shroud of Turin, which studies have shown was wrapped around the body of a seriously injured man whose heart was still beating.

But there are doctors who say the same when they consider that Jesus' wounds ran with blood and water. A third account attributed to the Essenians comes to the same conclusion, and in it, it is stated that care was taken of the body as soon as it was removed from the cross, wrapping it with bandages soaked in medicines that would heal the nearly fatal wounds. Afterwards, Jesus' body was taken to a safe place where he could recover.

Another hypothesis mentions the fact that Jesus knew techniques to induce voluntary catalepsy and thus feign death. His apostles would then have tended his wounds inside the large tomb and taken him out when night came. They must obviously have had the cooperation of the tomb guards.

The truth is within us

After offering a brief outline of these theories, we now return to the Gospels. The outcome of the Passion is the high point of the tragedy, the crucial moment of the prodigies. Matthew (27;51-56) presents it as follows:

And behold, the curtain of the temple was torn in two, from top to bottom; and the earth shook, and the rocks were split; the tombs also were opened, and many bodies of the saints who had fallen asleep were raised, and coming out of the tombs after his resurrection they went into the holy city and appeared to many. When the centurion and those who were with him, keeping watch over Jesus, saw the earthquake and what took place, they were filled with awe, and said, "Truly this was the Son of God!"

The burial of Jesus (drawing by Rembrandt)

"There were also many women there, looking on from afar, who had followed Jesus from Galilee, ministering to him; among whom were Mary Magdalene, and Mary the mother of James and Joseph, and the mother of the sons of Zebedee.

This is the most spectacular version offered by the four evangelists, while Mark says nothing except that the curtain

173

of the Temple split in two. If we believe this, we would have to suppose that this marked a moment in the life of Jerusalem, the 'Holy City' that would never be forgotten. None of this is recorded in the documents of the time, because such a sequence of extraordinary events did not take place.

Matthew uses symbols taken from the Old Testament. For example, the curtain of the Temple should be taken to mean that a new era is beginning, and that the cycle of the previous one had ended, and the Temple would be replaced by a new one. In the Letter to the Hebrews, this is interpreted as total regeneration with the past left behind, for Jesus had been sacrificed as the lamb on the altar.

The trembling of the earth, the splitting of the rocks and the resuscitation of the dead are also symbols from the Old Testament. They come to mean that the Son of God has been sacrificed, and from that moment the world is under judgement. The cosmos must then be shaken, even if this is only a figure of speech.

The coming of darkness can be accepted because of the lunar eclipse, and so too can certain disturbances in the weather.

Really, the interpretation of the death of Jesus is personal. Each of us has the right to value it according to the information he or she has at hand, and, especially, according to his or her own beliefs.

What others have said

This chapter would not be complete if we did not mention here that there are very competent historians, both in the West and in India and Egypt, who have written magnificent studies on why Jesus did not die on the cross. We have mentioned the Essenians who might have healed him inside the tomb, and then taken him to a place where he could completely recover.

An ancient Hindu sutra called Natha-nama-vali by the Indian Yogis gives a surprising version of Jesus' crucifixion, known as Isha Natha. The reference has been taken from the book *A Search for the Historical Jesus* by Fida Hassnain:

Isha Natha came to India when he was fourteen, and returned to his own country to preach. His brutish, materialistic compatriots soon began to conspire against him and eventually had him crucified. While he was on the cross, or perhaps even before, Isha Natha reached the samadhi or profound trance through yoga.

Seeing him in these conditions, the Jews believed him to be dead and took him to a tomb. At that moment, however, one of his gurus or masters, the great Chetan Natha, was on the slopes of the Himalayas immersed in deep meditation, and had a vision in which he saw the tortures that were being carried out on Isha Natha, and made his body light as air and was transported to the lands of Israel.

The day of his arrival was signalled by thunder and lightning in the rage of the Gods against the Jews, and the earth shook. When he arrived, Chetan Natha took Isha Natha's body from the tomb, woke him from his samadhi and then took him to the sacred lands of the Aryans. Then Isha Natha was established in an ashram in the lower regions near the Himalayas and there he established the cult of the lingam *and the* yoni.

This reference to the cult of the *lingam* and the *yoni* refers to the ancient fertility rites practised in the regions between the Tigris and Euphrates rivers that enclosed the lands of Mesopotamia.

The yogic version of Jesus' life seems to us to be extremely rich figuratively, especially in its use of the imagination. Here

175

we might remember the experience of a Russian explorer, Anton Bisyminski, who was lost in the Himalayas towards the beginning of the century. He nearly froze to death but was saved by lamas. After some months, seeing his anguish at not being able to walk, they asked him why he was so sad. When they heard that he could not stop thinking of his family whom he had not seen for the last two years, they placed him in front of a mirror where he could see all of his loved ones pruning rose bushes. He saw them as clearly as if they were right in front of him. Some time later, Bisyminski found out from the mouths of his family themselves that on that day, which they will never forget, they were actually pruning rose bushes.

In spite of all these mental prodigies of the lamas and yogis, we still believe that the valid version of the story is the one contained in the New Testament. But it is our obligation to recount what others say, and this is why we have presented such a singular story here.

CHAPTER XIV

THE RESURRECTION

Is it all a myth?

Certain historians dare to say that the life of Jesus life ended with his death, as the resurrection forms part of the legend or the apostles' desire for it to happen to endow their Master with godlike qualities. They do accept that the priests of Jerusalem were afraid that such a thing might happen, which is why they asked Pilate to place a guard before the sepulchre, as they were convinced that "after three days [he would] rise again."

The belief in resurrection on the third day after his death is from the Old Testament, and is taken from the time Jonas spent in the belly of the whale. Because Matthew the evangelist was so fond of making references to biblical texts, he used this to speak of a very debatable fact.

However, the Apocryphal Gospel of Peter, written halfway through the second century, contains the following passage:

Now in the night whereon the Lord's day dawned, as the soldiers were keeping guard two by two in every watch, there came a great sound in the heaven, and they saw the heavens opened and two men descend thence, shining with a great light, and drawing near unto the sepulchre. And that stone which had been set on the door rolled away of itself and went back to the side, and the sepulchre was opened and both of the young men entered in. When therefore those soldiers saw that, they waked up the centurion and the elders (for they also were there keeping watch); and while they were yet telling them the things which they had seen, they saw again three men come out of the sepulchre, and two of them sustaining the other, and a cross following, after them. And of the two they saw that their heads reached unto heaven, but of him that was led by them that it overpassed the heavens. And they heard a voice out of the heavens saying: Hast thou preached unto them that sleep? And an answer was heard from the cross, saying: Yea.

Those men therefore took counsel one with another to go and report these things unto Pilate. And while they yet thought thereabout, again the heavens were opened and a man descended and entered into the tomb. And they that were with the centurion when they saw that, hasted to go by night unto Pilate and left the sepulchre whereon they were keeping watch, and told all that they had seen, and were in great agony, saying: Of a truth he was the son of God.

The Apocryphal Gospel of Peter

We should mention here that the Apocryphal Gospels are not a negation of the four accepted ones. They often serve to give additional information, but at other times introduce confusing contradictions. The same, however, is true of the texts approved by the Church.

With regard to the passage taken out of the Apocryphal Gospel of Peter, this has been included to prove that Jesus Christ resuscitated from among the dead. The script is certainly poorly written, but it adds more information to the Gospel according to Matthew. When it mentions that the heads of the first two men (the angels) reached the heavens, and the head of the one who was led by them reached higher, it is clear that symbols are being used. If not, we would need to imagine three giants of monstrous proportions that would have invoked panic in the guards. The idea is that the first two were angels, while the third is to be considered superior to his companions for having earned the glory of God.

As an anecdote, we must remember that Jesus did not spend three days in the tomb, but rather two nights and a day. If the crucifixion happened on Friday at the ninth hour, three in the afternoon, and the resurrection on Sunday in the early morning, this can be calculated with ease. He was thus not 'entombed' for the three complete days that Jonas remained inside the belly of the whale.

One of the appearances of Jesus

Also, the fact that Jesus was resuscitated on a Sunday led the church to adopt it as their 'holy day', causing even greater rift between it and the Jews, whose Sabbath day is observed on Saturday.

The testimony of the Gospels

Perhaps the greatest differences between the gospels can be seen in the stories of the resurrection. All four authors mention that the tomb was found empty and that the risen Christ appeared; however, the events that led to the discovery of the tomb, the number, the place and the people who saw him when he appeared vary considerably from one account to the next.

The main discrepancies will be pointed out here. In the Gospel according to Matthew (28:1-10) we are told:

Now after the Sabbath, toward the dawn of the first day of the week, Mary Magdalene and the other Mary went to see the sepulchre. And behold, there was a great earthquake; for an angel of the Lord descended from heaven and came and rolled back the stone, and sat upon it. His appearance was like lightning, and his raiment white as snow. And for fear of him the guards trembled and became like dead men. But the angel said to the women, "do not be afraid; for I know that you seek Jesus who was crucified. He is not here; for he has risen, as he said. Come, see the place where he lay. Then go quickly and tell his disciples that he has risen from the dead, and behold, he is going before you to Galilee; there you will see him: Lo, I have told you." So they departed quickly from the tomb with fear and great joy, and ran to tell his disciples. And behold, Jesus met them and said, "Hail!" And they came up and took hold of his feet and worshiped him. Then Jesus said to them, "Do not be afraid; go and tell my brethren to go to Galilee, and there they will see me."

180

The version presented by Mark is fairly similar, though he leaves out the dramatic earthquake and does not clearly indicate if the man the women met was an angel. John also ignores the geological phenomenon, as well as the men guarding the tomb. In his version, Mary Magdalene finds the stone rolled aside from the entrance to the tomb, and is so frightened that she runs off to find Peter and James, who go into the tomb and encounter only the shrouds. Meanwhile, Mary waits outside and there she sees the two angels and then Jesus, whom she initially believes to be the gardener. Lastly, Jesus appears in the evening to his disciples in a closed room to show them his wounds so that they might believe.

Luke dwells less on the supernatural details in his story of the resurrection, only mentioning three women who go to the tomb and find it empty. Feeling disturbed, they see two men in shining clothes coming towards them to remind them that the 'Son of Man' has just risen on the third day as he had foretold. Next they go off to look for the apostles to tell them what has happened. But their listeners think they are delirious and do not believe them. But Peter goes nevertheless to have a look at the site, and when he comes to the empty tomb, decides that they are telling the truth.

There are such obvious differences in the versions and omissions of 'important' facts that we should certainly question the story told here.

As for the appearances of Jesus, the disparities become so exaggerated to form a single story out of the different gospels becomes a truly impossible task. Matthew, Mark and John's epilogue at least mention that these appearances took place in Jerusalem. Also, it is enough just to read the four gospels to discover the enormous discrepancies between the tales of his appearances, which in essence seem to be speaking of the same occurrence. We also have to take into account that one

181

evangelist might be telling of an appearance that the others did not know about – such as the appearance that Luke speaks of to the two disciples of Emmaus.

The validity of the testimonies

The exaggerated dissonances between the different versions of the evangelists regarding the resurrection of Jesus Christ would seem to be reason enough to doubt their historical validity. Reimarus opens his rationalist critique as follows:

Reader, you who are serious and a lover of the truth, tell me before God: Could you take a testimony that so clearly and frequently contradicts itself in its account of something so important, in details such as the people, the time, the way, the end, the words and the story, as unanimous and serious?

In spite of this comment, we believe that at the bottom of the story truth is to be found, and that the resurrection is an historical fact. This does not mean, however, that it is not full of issues which are difficult to establish. We must remember that the evangelists did not witness the event, but rather relied on the versions of others and wrote them down. Yet none of them were aware of what the others were writing, nor did they know of what other writers of the Apocryphal Gospels were saying. They lived in different environments and each of them wrote for a specific audience. We should mention the 'truth revealed', but this would lead to even more confusion, as we would have to deduce that the revelation came to the writers through very different means, because if there had only been one there would not be so many variations and contradictions in their accounts.

The importance of the empty tomb

Jesus was buried by Joseph of Arimathea, an 'important member of the Sanhedrin' who used his position to get Pilate's immediate permission. An isolated tomb was chosen, when the normal practice was to bury the crucified in a common grave. This must be seen as a privilege allowed to Joseph. The fact that all of the evangelists mention this crucial name is considered to be definitive proof of its validity, as otherwise they could have mentioned no one or given different names.

Did Jesus appear to Peter when he was a fisherman once again?

The Jews doubted that Jesus had been buried in an isolated tomb. However, in 1968, archaeologists discovered some tombs in the north of Jerusalem, and in one of them found the remains of a victim of crucifixion, whose heel bones had been pierced through with an iron nail. The tibia had also been intentionally broken. They found pottery in the same place from the time of Jesus. This proved that some victims of crucifixion were buried in separate tombs.

The evangelists say that the women were the first to discover that the tomb was empty, and this was a risk, as the Jews did not accept women as witnesses at a trial. The fact that they are the ones to give testimony to the resurrection makes it more believable.

The appearances of Jesus

In the stories of the appearances, each of the evangelists again goes his own way. However, if we ignore the obvious differences, all of the versions coincide in the basic testimony that the disciples believed they saw Jesus resurrected after his death. We shall leave aside the literary or historical problems arising here for the time being to concentrate on the fundamental content of the texts, i.e. the affirmation of these men that they saw Jesus alive after his death.

We deliberately mention that the gospels provide us with a reliable testimony that faith in Christ's resurrection originates from the fact that some men believe they saw him. Now, even among critics who will not admit the resurrection, there are very few who deny that the apostles "believed they saw Jesus"; that is, they had experiences that can be clearly designated 'visions' or 'apparitions'. This is not any kind of aberration.

The problem lies in trying to determine exactly what kind of phenomenon we are speaking of here. Were they real visions of the Risen Christ; in other words, visions with an external source that appear to men, or were they simple projections from the unconscious?

The former idea is supported by the traditional interpretation of the Church: Jesus resurrected, living in the glory of his Father, becoming visible to his followers. In the latter we have what we might call the traditional interpretation of rationalist critique: the disciples could not believe that Jesus' work had ended with his death on the cross, and this spiritual need of theirs caused the idea arise in them that their Master had not remained dead, but was still alive. In other words, the 'apparitions' arose from men's desires and became natural phenomena to them.

One way of reconstructing the facts

One possible version of events is offered by C. Guignebert:

After Jesus' death, Peter returned to his home to Capernaum. He was prepared to take up fishing again in the boat he had so often used to take Jesus from one side of the lake to the other. Reminders of his days of hope and glory were everywhere before his eyes. The image of the Master followed him wherever he went, filling the framework of his life. His spirit was fixed on one thought: this could not have ended; something had to happen, and it would happen through Him; he was not fooling himself, for it was impossible that He had abandoned them; he would have to appear soon. And while the pain at losing Jesus grew in him and his exasperation grew as his hope did not materialise, his confidence in the coming miracle and the manifestation of Christ in person grew stronger and more exalted. We should not then be surprised that Peter eventually saw Jesus. Where? Probably on the lakeshore, in conditions where this could easily hap-

*pen: in the morning haze or the dazzle of the midday sun.
Perhaps Peter was alone at the time, but there is no need to
imagine this either: he might have been able to gather some
of the best disciples around him, the Twelve; and it would
have been normal for them to see Him too. In this kind of happening the only really difficult thing is for the initiative to
arise. Once it does the rest comes easily, and contagion is the
general rule. Here, it was easy for contagion to take place,
for Peter's companions were in a similar state of mind to him.*

To this reconstruction of the events, of which there are
other similar versions, we say: the historical facts that we
possess make it completely impossible. First of all, the dura-
tion of the appearances contradicts it. If the New Testament
only spoke of one appearance to a person or group, or of
appearances on one day only, the hypothesis of a subjective
hallucinatory phenomenon might be acceptable. But the
sources speak of repeated appearances over a long period of
time, and a hallucination or a sustained string of hallucinations over such a long time are even more incomprehensible
than the traditional interpretation that evokes manifestations
of the glorious Christ.

Those who try to explain subjective visions in such radically different men after the sad end Jesus' cause came to as
natural phenomena have to use psychological constructs, as
we have seen in the writings of C. Guibnebert. Such types of
explanation abound. An amazing level of fantasy can be seen
here even in normally sober, sensible theoreticians' work.
The rationalistic view of G. Lohfink is more sensible, however:

*All these constructions coincide in one affirmation: that
faith sprung in the disciples' hearts, and that faith produces
visions. But, according to the New Testament, what happens*

186

is just the opposite: it is the appearances of the Risen Christ themselves that make faith in the resurrection possible. It is inconceivable that a serious historian could twist such a clear affirmation from his or her sources – especially the personal testimony of Saint Paul – and read exactly the opposite into them.

Regarding the hallucinations

There is another extremely important consideration to be made here. In hallucinatory phenomena or purely psychogenic projections, certain conditions need to found in the subject in order for them to take place. Someone who does not believe in the devil or anything like him will never think they have seen the devil. If Jesus' disciples came to believe in the resuscitation of their Master with no objective reason to do so, and the visions produced were purely a question of a previous belief, then it was necessary for this belief, or even a strong need, to exist in them beforehand. We shall now see how this predisposition did not exist in them.

As we have said, what the apostles were publicly proclaiming just after Jesus' death was not his return to his previous life, but that God had resuscitated him and that this was the beginning of the resurrection of all the dead. They were Jewish and therefore shared the beliefs of Judaism in the resurrection of the dead.

However, the apostles preached that the resurrection of the dead had begun, and that the resurrection of Jesus Christ marked the beginning of the end of the world and the new creation. There is no similar belief to this in Judaism, nor in any of the Greek religions that might be a starting point for Christianity. We do have stories of resurrections of the dead in which they come back to the life that death interrupted.

But the resurrection that the apostles predicted for Jesus is radically different.

The Ascension

In Jewish tradition several men had been taken to heaven, such as Enoch and Elijah. If Jesus' disciples did not accept having lost their Master forever, according to the hypothesis of the hallucinations, then this Jewish tradition would have given them the perfect disposition to think that Jesus had been taken to heaven.

But, as we insist, what these men were proclaiming was not that Jesus had been taken to heaven or ascended, but that the resurrection of the dead, thought by the Jews to be an event marking the end of Humankind, was beginning with him. As G. Lohfink says:

To attribute the birth of this belief to an evolution in the religious ideas of those who profess it is extraordinarily improbable. It cannot be explained how men who came out of the Jewish tradition could conceive the beginning of the end times only for Jesus.

According to Jewish tradition, the resurrection of the dead would affect all human beings, and would not take place until the end of the world.

We can finish off, then, with an assertion: the way the primitive Church explained the message regarding the resurrection is to make it come from a real experience, not a purely subjective one, of the resurrection of Jesus seen by the first witnesses, described in the Gospels. With this we do not wish to say that historical research can enlighten us as to the mystery of Jesus' resurrection, as this can only be done by faith. But what it can allow is for us to leave the form of each person's belief in the mystery of this work of God to each person according to his or her moral principles.

A conclusion that is not one...

We shall end this biography on Jesus leaving it at a key moment: proving that he was the Son of God. This is where we finish; it is our conclusion. There are others, certainly, and these form part of the beliefs of our readers.

The Ascension of Jesus to heaven

What we have decided to make very clear is that Jesus was a Man, the greatest that ever existed, who preached a doctrine of universal relevance. If the materialists were sincere they would recognise that the roots of Human Rights, of pure communism and other democratic political ideologies are inspired in the Gospels. For nobody defended the humble, the 'proletariat' as Jesus did — he lived with them and adopted their clothing, their customs and their way of thinking. He converted workers and patrons who were also grappling for their existence (fishing in the boats with their employees) in his disciples, and confronted the establishment for the good of the lower classes.

Who before Jesus had dared to preach that the King and the humblest of men were equal? Whose voice dared to uncover the hypocrisy of the ruling classes before their main representatives?

Only other enlightened men such as Buddha, Confucius and Pythagoras had done this before, but none so strongly as Jesus and at the cost of his life . What the Church did later with Jesus' doctrine is another matter, which would require many books to discuss. We believe that Jesus himself, the Jewish son of a carpenter and the unforgettable Mary, would not recognise the image given of Him by the Vatican if he were to return to Earth. But he would feel comfortable in other areas of the world where missionaries, members of different international organisations and other altruistic agencies are putting their lives, knowledge and spirit into helping the underprivileged of the earth, because Jesus preached the most absolute universal, unconditional, selfless equality. His was not a political doctrine or even a religion, since the most important thing for him was infinite love towards all men and women in the world, both in his time and later times until the end of time.

INDEX

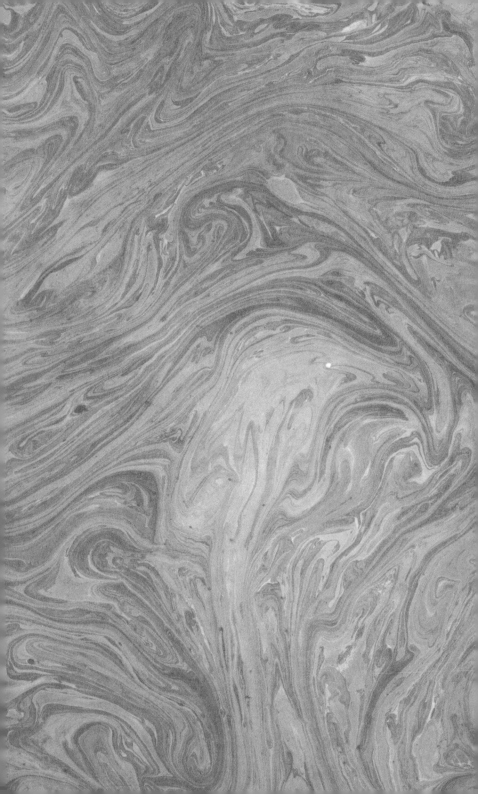